MW01172743

A Good Day To Die

What 276 executions taught a death row chaplain about life

Carina Bergfeldt

Translation by Alice Menzies
Editing by Kerstin Ödeen
Cover design: Emilie Ekström
Photographer: Pontus Orre

For Jim.

Thank you for sharing your life with me.

Our Last Conversation
December 2021

"Maybe you should wait until I'm dead to publish this book."
 I don't know why it feels so important to have a record of this, but I glance down to make sure the Dictaphone is still running. I then turn to him in the brown leather recliner where he has spent hour after hour, day after day, surrounded by the decorations his wife has put up. There are nine faux Christmas trees of varying sizes in this room alone.

What makes you say that?

He looks up at the wooden cross on the wall—an object he has told me several times now was made by a prisoner—and hesitates for a moment before he answers.
 "I'm a man of God. The confidences I've broken, the things I've done, everything I told you... I'm not sure how people will feel about all that. I just think it might be for the best if I'm not around when it comes out."

Our First Conversation
July 2013

Pastor Jim Brazzil looks down at the stack of pancakes the waitress has just served us. They're drenched in whipped cream and piled high with strawberries. The hash browns are swimming in grease, as is the mound of bacon. But that isn't all. We also have scrambled eggs, an omelet, two mugs of hot coffee, and a couple of large lemonades with plenty of ice—Texas-style.

He laughs and asks whether we're really going to eat all of this.

I assure him that we are.

I met Jim Brazzil for the first time at a Denny's in the city of Huntsville, Texas. I've come to the U.S. to work on a series of articles under the heading of "A Week with Death" for the Swedish newspaper *Aftonbladet*, and as we sit down, only a few hours have passed since I met Vaughn Ross, a death row inmate at the Polunsky Unit. Ross has seven days left to live, and I plan to spend the week leading up to his execution meeting with people whose work brings them into contact with the death penalty in various ways. The pastor in front of me, a retired prison chaplain, is one of them.

My conversation with Ross, who was sentenced to death for double homicide, is still weighing heavily on my mind as we sit down to eat. I told the pastor that he and I had talked about books and that he had just finished *The Alchemist* by Paulo Coelho. I shared that I had recently read another title by the same author, *The Devil and Miss Prym*, about a man who offers the inhabitants of a town a chest full of gold in exchange for selecting one person to die and that the book shows what people are really capable of when push comes to shove.

"I want to read that book!" Ross told me, though he immediately grew pensive and corrected himself: "I would have liked to read it."

Jim nods. He knows where my story is heading.

"The library cart on death row only comes around once a week," he says.

And we both know where Vaughn Ross will be seven days from now: in the death chamber—the green room, which is the reason we're having this conversation at all. The place no one wants to visit, but which Jim Brazzil knows better than most.

Vaughn Ross will never get to read *The Devil and Miss Prym*.

For years, the pastor was the last person to touch or speak to condemned prisoners before they slipped out of consciousness and died. He sat with 154 convicted killers before they were given the lethal injection, and he also assisted in one execution involving Yellow Mama, Alabama's infamous electric chair. Jim Brazzil watched a further 121 people die from the witness room alongside the victims' relatives—276 people in total.

Two hours pass and the pancakes are long gone. The waitress cleared away what was left of the bacon and eggs, and we were both on our third cup of coffee.

Speaking to someone like Jim Brazzil, time seems to pull you into a kind of dance. In his presence, you feel the here and now—the there and then. His stories swirl around the table, and all you can do is join in. You're ten years old and have just been given a death sentence. You expect to die before your twelfth birthday, but you're so young and curious about life that what you really want is to live and serve God. You're locked in a cell. You're in an execution chamber with your hand on a murderer's ankle. You're listening to a final confession. The hours we spend together flit between life and death. Faith and hope. Joy and sorrow. Memories and confessions.

Jim lives a normal, everyday life—just another aging conservative from Texas—and yet I'm practically transfixed by everything he tells me, by the life he has lived. It's time we wrapped up our interview, but neither of us makes any attempt to get up.

I ask what I think will be my last question.

How have those 276 executions affected your own attitude toward death?

. . .

10

Jim Brazzil smiles. I can tell from his eyes that he is considering his words carefully, but after a moment or two, it's as though he has made up his mind. The former chaplain leans forward.

"I'd like to say one more thing."

What he tells me pushes the story in another direction. It transforms him from someone I wanted to interview for background information into the main focus of this book—it's just that neither of us realizes it at the time.

"In some ways, I understand what they're going through, these folks who've been sentenced to death. I have prostate cancer and stage four leukemia, a death sentence of my own. Seven years ago, they told me I had five years left to live. That's why I stopped attending the executions. My body won't last much longer. It's my turn to die."

He is quiet.

I am quiet.

Oblivious to her bad timing, the waitress comes over and asks if we'd like more coffee. I nod, and she fills our cups for the fourth time. I'm trying to determine whether what he told me was off the record or whether I can write about it.

And so I ask.

Jim says I'm welcome to use it.

"Death is death," he continues. "What this job has taught me, and what this illness has really emphasized, is that so many people waste their lives. And I don't necessarily mean the guys on death row. I've seen witnesses to executions who haven't been able to take a single step since the day their loved one died. People who've been in a trance for ten, fifteen, twenty years, filled with hate."

He pauses and takes a sip of coffee before he goes on.

"What almost three hundred executions have taught me is that those men and women were alive one minute and dead the next. I'm going to die too. When I do, I'll take with me the same message I shared with them, which I'd love for you to pass on. And that's that life is a blessing. Don't waste it. Do good whenever you can and forgive whatever you can forgive. And once you've done that, move on, whether it's in this life or the next."

Two hours later, our breakfast/lunch is finally over, and we're out in the parking lot. Rather than heading our separate ways, we decide to drive over to Joe Byrd Cemetery. Jim Brazzil tells me it's his favorite place in Huntsville, and he wants me to see it.

The former chaplain gets into his enormous blue pickup and drives away, but I sit in my rental car for a moment, trying to gather the thoughts swirling around my head.

He has faced so much poison over the course of his life, so much sadness and evil, and now his body is full of a different sort of poison. I know that isn't how it works, but I do wonder whether there could be a link between what he has had to deal with spiritually and what his body has gone through physically—and to have done it all with such calm.

Jim Brazzil talks about reconciliation, but I don't want to forgive. He talks about peace, but I'm so angry. He says life is a blessing, but I'm not living; I'm surviving. He says people should move forward and move on, but I don't feel like I ever consciously act. All I do is react.

In my mind's eye, I see a young girl hiding in her father's garage, waiting for his rage to pass. I see clenched fists and hear the dull sound of punches. A ten-year-old with a knife in her hand, ready to use it.

There are people in my life I have no intention of ever forgiving, and I'm angry with God for giving the man I just met a death sentence.

He doesn't deserve it. Other people do.

Sitting there, I do something I've never done before during all my years as a reporter.

I lean forward against the wheel, and I cry.

I don't know if it's for him or for me.

Maybe it's for both of us.

Captain Joe Byrd Cemetery really is one of the most beautiful places in Huntsville, though for a long time, it was anything but. For many years, it was a muddy scrap of land full of anthills and weeds.

The cemetery is less than a mile from the prison, on a quiet slope just off Bowers Boulevard in the older area of town. The land was donated to the governor in 1855, and due to a misunderstanding, the authorities soon began burying prisoners there. With the damage already done, the decision was made to continue digging graves on the site, and the cemetery has been known locally as Peckerwood Hill ever since.

Peckerwood—an inversion of 'woodpecker'—is the name that was given to poor prisoners in the past. A nickname used to describe the same group of uneducated white people now known as white trash. Those who had no one willing or able to pay for them to be laid to rest—irritating wood-peckers.

According to Texas state law, anyone who dies while incarcerated has the right to a proper burial, regardless of what they were convicted of—even if there is no one to pay for it. These men and women end up on Peckerwood Hill, which is currently the final resting place of over three thousand Huntsville prisoners. Many of them are buried in graves that do not bear their name—nothing put a prisoner number and an X indicating that they were executed. In the 1960s, however, acting Warden Joe Byrd decided that this was so undignified that he began to go to the cemetery on his days off to tidy up the grounds. Over time, he was helped by a handful of trusted prisoners, and they created the beautiful cemetery as it is today. The authorities have yet to determine the identities of the people buried in 312 of the old graves, but these days, the prisoners' final resting places are marked with their names on simple white crosses made by the other inmates. Burials take place every Thursday—providing someone has died during the preceding week—and on the day after an execution unless the relatives have claimed the body.

I'm trying to work out whether I think this would be a good place to be laid to rest for all eternity when I spot Jim Brazzil coming toward me.

"I wouldn't have anything against being buried here," he says, as though he has read my mind.

We walk around the cemetery together. Jim Brazzil committed five hundred people to the earth here during his time as a prison chaplain, and he points out a few individuals he remembers particularly well. He describes the strange, sad feeling when no one else turned up to pay their respects, when the only people present were himself and a prison representative. How undignified he found it that the person in question had no one to grieve them—though he also understood that many of them deserved to have had their family and society turn their backs on them.

Jim tells me about a burial he led for a man who died in prison. A handful of others were in attendance that day. Jim had never met him since the man hadn't been on death row. He told the people gathered around the grave that they were welcome to say a few words if they wished. There was an awkward silence, and then a young man stepped forward and looked down into the hole.

"I'm only here because I want to make sure the son-of-a-bitch is really dead," he said. "He was my old man, and he abused me."

I often fantasize about my father's funeral. Walking up to the front of the church, standing at the altar, and verbally tearing him to pieces with the most brutal farewell speech imaginable. I've dreamed about it for years now. Decades.

Jim Brazzil studies me.

"Is that so?"

He doesn't ask anything else; he doesn't need to. In that moment, I get a glimpse of how easy it is to share things you hadn't meant to with Jim Brazzil and how liberating it is to confess to something shameful and be met with nothing but compassion.

Jim moves on, pointing to another grave and reminiscing about another burial. At the end of the ceremony, a young boy—no older than three or four—runs forward. He drops his pants and starts peeing on the coffin.

"I was totally blindsided, but no one did anything to stop him. It turned out none of them had especially fond feelings toward the boy's grandfather. They probably all wanted to do the same."

He keeps going, wandering between the graves. Jim draws my attention to seven rows of twelve crosses and tells me he buried every single one. He also tells me about a day he ministered at five funerals during a heavy snowstorm. None of the dead men's relatives were in attendance. Jim Brazzil drove into the cemetery and heard the snow and the wind whistling around his car. The prison warden told him that he didn't need to get out and that he could conduct the ceremony from the car if he wanted to.

The pastor shakes his head at the memory.

"I couldn't do that to them."

We reach five old graves marked with women's names, and Jim Brazzil tells me that each of them has been moved. He was present during the exhumations to bless the dead in their new resting places. He points to one and asks me not to write the woman's name. Her coffin broke during the move, and her dead body fell to the ground.

"It was awful. It happened in the blink of an eye. She wasn't wearing any clothes, either. Just a shroud. And since that had come off, she was completely naked. The men charged with moving the coffins were all inmates, and they stared down at her. After a moment, one of them whispered: 'That there's a vagina. I ain't seen one of those in ten years. Typical—when I finally get to see one, it's been dead fifty years.'"

The chaplain starts laughing.

"Sorry, I can't help it. That was one of the most grotesque, tragicomic things I ever went through here."

. . .

Standing beneath a tree, Jim Brazzil looks all around. There are graves, as far as the eye can see, in every direction, none decorated with flowers—so many men who have died in Texas's prisons, so few people who grieve them. For a few seconds, it's as though he is seeing the cemetery for the first time.

"This is a beautiful place, but it's also an unhappy one. I like it, though. I've spent a lot of time here."

We reach some of the oldest graves, five of which bear the same date: February 18, 1924.

"These five were the first to be executed using Old Sparky. Five executions in a row. They sat down in the electric chair one after another."

He points to one of the graves. The dead man's name is Melvin Johnson.

"Funny. I was present at the execution of another Melvin Johnson."

The sun is high in the sky, and birds are singing in the trees. So many things keep bringing back memories, including the beautiful weather. Jim Brazzil tells me about one inmate who got out of the vehicle that transported him to Huntsville and looked up at the sun, which he hadn't seen in twelve years. He enjoyed its warm rays on his face for a moment, then turned to the chaplain, smiled, and said, "It's a good day to die."

Jim Brazzil raises his own face to the sky and lets the sun warm his cheeks.

"Today would also be a good day to die if that turned out to be the case. I've done everything I need to do."

. . .

What do you say to the prisoners right before they die?

"I say thank you for sharing your life with me."

That's when it hits me: he isn't done yet.

Your life should be a book. It would be such a shame if the things you've told me today disappeared with you when you leave this world.

He chuckles.

"Did you know that I turned down a million dollars from a movie company that wanted to do just that? Warner Brothers, that was it. They wanted to make a book and a TV show about my life in the nineties. Not that I didn't want the money—Lord knows I could have done with it—but they wanted to change certain things, make me out to be a hero. But I'm not a hero."

We say our goodbyes, and he looks me in the eye and smiles.

"Today was a special day, wasn't it? I talked about things I've never talked about before."

Me too.

I fly back to Sweden.

My series of articles on death row and the execution of Vaughn Ross are read by 2.2 million Swedes—a quarter of the population—and a year later, I re-work those texts into a book, *Seven Days to Live*.

Days become months, which become years, and I continue to write about death and suffering. Whenever I'm given the choice, I focus on gang rapes in India and murdered girls along a highway in Canada. The darkness becomes my friend. These are the assignments I feel most comfortable working on and the jobs I do best. I'm not sure why, but the vulnerable have always found it easy to open up to me.

I travel back to Texas, just two hours from Huntsville. This time, I went there to interview David Smither. He was nine when his twelve-year-old sister Laura disappeared after going out for a jog. Twenty years have passed by the time we meet, but her killer has not been brought to justice.

David tells me about the trauma of losing a sibling and how he essentially became an orphan the day his sister died. He tells me how his parents' grief caused them to forget about him and how he learned not to talk, not to feel, and not to trust anyone.

When I finish my piece, I offer to translate it for him so he can hear what I've written. I sit beside him in a hotel room in Texas City and read about the young David's grief, loneliness, and vulnerability. Once I'm done, he looks me in the eye and says the boy in him feels seen and comforted for the first time.

His words cause something inside me to break, and in that moment, I understand precisely why I am always drawn to the darkness. Sitting beside this young man with tears in his eyes, prompted by my piece about his childhood, I find myself thinking about my own life. About the young girl who never had any articles written about her, who learned not to talk about it, not to feel, not to trust anyone, the child who was never comforted.

With that, I also realize why I always seek out victims in my work. It's because I never have to work to win their trust. It comes naturally because we share a certain kinship. And, as so many times before, I find myself thinking about Jim Brazzil.

I think about his innate calmness despite everything he has been through, the forgiveness he has shown so many people who didn't believe they deserved it, and his acceptance of the fact that life is as it is and was as it was. I want to experience some of that—some of his calmness, acceptance, and forgiveness. Right now, it feels like I don't have any.

I let a little more time pass, but in the end, I just can't resist any longer. I have to try. I dial Jim's number, and he tells me he has been waiting for my call.

I can't offer you millions of dollars, but if I promise not to make you into a hero, would you consider sharing your life story with me?

"Yes," he says. "I'd like that very much."

And so, I bought a plane ticket and returned to Texas.

Chapter One

Now

One hundred and fifty-five. That is how many times Jim Brazzil has sat with someone facing a death sentence. Listening to stories in life's final moments, when everything comes surging out, and people feel a need to share.

One hundred and fifty-five times as the other person in the room.

One hundred and fifty-five times as me.

But he is now the condemned man, ready to make his deathbed confession.

And I am him, the person whose job it is to listen.

He's a little nervous, and so am I.

The plan is to spend two weeks together. I have a room half an hour from his house at a two-star motel that feels like something out of a movie with its red carpet and satin bedspread. I've bought a microphone and a Dictaphone, and we're trying to find a good place to clip the mic on his yellow shirt. He is half-sprawled on the sofa in his office, allowing him to stretch out and ease the aches from his cancer treatment. Jim laughs and tells me it reminds him of a therapist's couch. Not that he has ever spent any time on one of those; his job has always been to be the therapist.

I hit record for the first time.

"Where should I start?" he asks.

Chapter Two

For the first time in my life,
as a chaplain on death row, I was no longer mediocre.

September 1995

The prison warden looks the chaplain straight in the eye.

"What we need is for him to die. What we need is to keep him calm until he dies. How you do that is up to you."

Jim Brazzil holds his new boss's gaze and says, "Okay."

"This is an incredibly important time," the warden continues. "We're counting on you. You need to spiritually prepare him for death. You need to get him to talk to you. To trust you. You need to do whatever it takes to keep him calm; that's your job here. Do it in a way that meets his needs and ours."

Four days have passed since Jim got the call from his old boss, asking him to come to Huntsville at eight a.m. on

Monday, September 11, 1995. He didn't say why, just that they could discuss it then—and that Jim would need two suits.

There are a lot of prisons in Texas, but it is the Walls Unit—as Huntsville is also known—that carries out the state's executions. Over the past 200 years, Texas has gone from hanging to the electric chair to an outright ban and then to the lethal injection. Between 1819 and 1923, the various counties were responsible for carrying out their own executions by hanging, some 390 in total, without any real involvement from the state. In 1923, however, the decision was made to transfer all executions to Huntsville and to use the electric chair. The workmen tasked with building Old Sparky were serving prison sentences themselves, and their chair took the lives of 361 inmates before a thirty-year-old by the name of Joseph Johnson Jr. became the last man to die in it on July 30, 1964.

This was followed by twelve years of heated debate, and the Supreme Court considered the question of whether the death penalty caused unnecessary suffering to the condemned and whether the sentence was handed down arbitrarily. Between 1972 and 1976, the death penalty was outlawed in the United States, and the fifty-two men awaiting execution in Texas had their sentences commuted to life imprisonment.

But the American people weren't happy. Public opinion was strong, and in 1976, the death penalty was reinstated following efforts to follow the Supreme Court's orders and tighten up regulations governing how and when the sentence could be handed down. In an attempt to minimize suffering, the states also began using lethal injection rather than the electric chair.

Jim Brazzil knew all this when he arrived at the prison that day—albeit vaguely.

"I showed up at my boss Jerry Groom's office that Monday morning in a brown pinstripe suit and a yellow and brown tie. He told me that the chaplain at Walls Unit had resigned with immediate effect and that they didn't have anyone else to take his place."

Because the correctional facility where Jim was supposed to work had yet to open, the boss wanted him to step in until they could find a replacement.

"He said, 'By the way, there's an execution scheduled for this evening. You'll have to take care of it. Can you handle an execution?'"

Jim Brazzil replied that he could certainly try, and with that, he set off for the prison that executes more inmates than any other in the whole of the United States. Upon his arrival, he met the warden.

"Warden Hodges said, 'Come with me, and I'll show you the death house,' which is where all the executions take place. I'd never been there before. He explained the process as we walked."

Jim found the Walls Unit spooky.

"It was built in 1848, and it has a different feel from any of the other prisons in Texas—and I've been to them all. Walls is different. It smells different. It *feels* different."

He inhales sharply through his nose as though he remembers its scent.

"It smells old. In my mind, I can still feel the vibrations

and the history. All the people and the stories that have been through that place. All the tragedy, sadness, and pain; everything that's been lost there. But at the same time, you can see the evolution of Texas in that building."

The warden gave Jim a guided tour of the facilities he would come to know exceptionally well.

Behind one of the doors he opened, there was a small garden with a neat lawn, white gardenias, pink lilies, and lush fig trees. It felt like a world away from the prison itself.

"Standing there, it was so hard to believe that I was surrounded by killers and rapists; it was all so beautiful."

The East Building, the original prison structure from 1848, was at one end of the garden. It had been in use for over 150 years, but it still filled the same function it was built for: housing inmates during their final hours of life.

When the East Building was first constructed, it had no external walls—nothing but the cells themselves and a flat roof.

"You had this enormous thirty-foot wall behind you and another in front of you, which made it feel like you were being crushed. Walking over there, you could see the huge chain-link fence, and it was like you were being taken deeper and deeper into the prison. It felt like you'd lost control and didn't know what was happening. We went in through the gates and over to the three doors in the far corner."

The prison warden opened one of them, which led into the execution chamber itself.

"I didn't know it at the time, but I would accompany 154 men and women through that door. There was a certain smell in that room; I can't really describe it. It smelled like old paint, and it smelled like death. I can't describe it any other way. It just smelled like death. There was another door to the room where they kept the generator for Old Sparky—though the chair is in the Huntsville Prison Museum these days."

Warden Hodges went into more detail about how the process worked, explaining, "We bring the inmate in, strip him, and search him. We then take his prints and put him in the cell. After that, we hand him over to you."

It was just before 9:00 in the morning, and the prisoner was due to arrive between 10:30 and 11:00.

"I remember thinking I had no idea what I would do once he arrived. And then we went into the death chamber itself, and I walked around the gurney and stood with my hands on it. I tried to imagine what it would feel like to have him strapped down there, looking up at the people in the witness room. There was only one side room like that at the time, which was for the inmate's family. The victim's relatives weren't allowed to observe executions back then—not until later."

That was when the warden looked Jim Brazzil in the eye and gave him the instructions he would remember for the rest of his life: that his job was to prepare the prisoners to die so that the state of Texas could execute them in as calm a manner as possible.

As the clock approached ten, they were back in the warden's office. The phone rang.

The execution had been postponed.

"Thank the Lord. I was so relieved. I don't know who was happier: me or the inmate."

The warden told Jim that he would like him to stay a few

days all the same, that the unit was in desperate need of a chaplain.

"He said to take a look around the chapel and the chaplain's office to get a feel for what it would be like, that there were a lot of inmates already waiting to speak to me."

With the words "your job is to take care of them," the prison warden left the new chaplain to it.

"I was really scared, though at the same time, I was excited to be there because it's such a historic place. I never imagined working somewhere like that; I'd always thought it must take someone exceptional to do that kind of job. I remember going to a ministerial meeting once, and my predecessor at the prison was there. I looked at him and thought, 'Man, he must be so talented to be able to do that job.' I really put him on a pedestal. I put the job on a pedestal, too."

Jim left the warden's office and took a look around.

Just outside, there was a so-called bullring with bars made from brass. It was the job of the oldest prisoners, those not capable of doing anything else, to clean and polish them.

On either side of the bullring, there were two small rooms. One was used for meetings between the inmates and their lawyers, and the other for reviewing the various procedures ahead of release.

A locked gate led through a desk known as the front desk, though for obvious reasons, no one managed to get that far into the prison without prior authorization. From there, a corridor ran over to the West Building, where some five hundred inmates were housed. Turning right led to the inner yard.

"Directly to the left of the yard, there's an impressive red brick building with a pretty steeple. Climbing the steps leads you straight into the chapel."

When Jim entered the chapel for the first time that day, he met Lisa Fields, who would be his assistant for the next six years.

"A Black lady, around fifteen years younger than me, she was very friendly, very cordial, and very smartly dressed. We sat down to talk, and she told me that she took care of the paperwork and that sort of thing. We chatted for a few minutes, and then I went to the chaplain's office alone."

The office had wooden walls, which were old pine with polyurethane varnish. Over the years, the boards had turned a deep yellow, and the carpet was red.

"It had such a unique scent, that old pine—like nothing I ever experienced before. I felt at home right away. It felt comfortable—like I was safe in there. I can't explain why, but I did."

Jim moved over to the desk and checked the drawers. He had expected them to be full of files, but there was nothing inside. No pens. No papers. No documents, paperclips, or hole punches. They were all completely empty, drawer after drawer. When the previous chaplain quit, he took everything with him—including five TVs, a DVD player, a VHS, and a P.A. system.

"That wasn't exactly the done thing if I can put it like that, but he'd been there so long that no one said anything."

The rumor that a new chaplain had arrived spread like wildfire, and Jim found himself busy all afternoon.

"People just kept on coming. Whenever someone new starts in a place like that, the inmates always want to see what they can get away with. They were hoping for an extra phone call or something along those lines because the chaplain was in charge of the ninety-day schedule."

This was in the days before pay phones were installed. If prisoners behaved, they were allowed to make a five-minute call every ninety days. The facility had 1,500 inmates at the time, and each one had the right to use the phone.

"That meant supervising between ten to fifteen phone calls daily, and I had to pay attention to everything they said. Most of it was desperation and longing—people who'd been inside a long time, wishing they could get out."

He laughs.

"There was one guy who had five wives. They lived on a farm together, all five of them plus the kids. We used to give him a little extra time so that he could say a few words to each one."

Eavesdropping on the inmates' calls was a big part of the job, as was choir practice. The prison had a Catholic choir and a Protestant choir, and Jim also held a Bible study group.

"There was always something going on in the chapel. We had to keep on top of who was there and when because no one was allowed to be there without our permission. That meant keeping multiple balls in the air, but I got used to it and learned the ropes pretty quickly."

The first thing Jim did was to get rid of the pulpit, one of only a handful of things the previous chaplain had left behind. His years as a minister in a Baptist church, where the pastor typically moves around rather than standing still, had left their mark on him, and he wanted to continue doing the same in prison.

Jim's first sermon got a lukewarm response from the inmates. They were used to the previous chaplain, who had been at the prison for twenty-two years.

"It was tough—that adjustment—because I was very different from him. I was still new; I did things by the book. But folks in prison don't like people who follow the rules."

Eight days after Jim began at the Walls Unit, another execution was scheduled to take place: a man from Fort Worth.

"When they arrive with the inmate, they drive through a tunnel and then out into what's known as the yard. I remember standing outside to wait for them. It was still morning, a warm day, and my head started spinning as I watched the van approach. I don't know how to explain it, but knowing that this was his last day on earth, that his life would soon be over, and that mine would change forever.... What was I going to say to him? How do you talk to someone who's about to be executed?"

Death wasn't new to Jim; he had met plenty of people who were dying over the years. But not like this. He tells me it felt strange to watch the man get out of the van with a chain connecting his hands and feet to his waist, meaning he could barely move.

"It was all so rigid. He stood tall and looked up at the sky before he shuffled into the death house."

One door after another slammed shut behind him, accompanied by the sound of keys turning in locks, taking him deeper and deeper into the building.

"It's a weird feeling to hear all those doors being locked."

The process started with a strip search, which involved

the inmate taking off all of his clothes. The inmate was made to examine himself while the officers watched, looking for weapons or other prohibited items. Once the search was over, someone tossed him a pair of underpants, which he pulled on. They then took his fingerprints, gave him some paper towels and a bar of soap, and took him to his cell.

"Until that moment, I hadn't said a word to him. I just hung back, watching. But once they put him in the cell, everyone but me and three of the guards left. I don't think he'd even noticed my presence at that point, even though I was standing right there on the other side of the bars. He went over to the sink and washed his hands. He dried them, and then he put on the clothes that had been left for him on his bunk."

Jim asked the condemned man whether he would like a cup of coffee, and the inmate said yes.

"I got him a cup and passed it through the bars. I knew the warden would be back soon, but I said, 'My name is Jim Brazzil. I'm the chaplain here.' I held my hand out to him, and he looked at me like I was crazy and refused to shake it. I tried to show him I meant it as a peaceful gesture, so I reached a little further in, and in the end, he took it. He had a good, firm handshake. We chatted a little after that, mostly about the drive from the Ellis Unit, where the death row inmates are housed."

The man said it had been fine and felt like it had taken forever to arrive. Jim asked whether he had been treated with respect, and he said he had.

That was roughly when the warden arrived, accompanied by the entourage that always surrounded him on such occasions: the associate warden, the major, and the press spokesperson.

"He came with a whole bunch of people. My job was to introduce the warden to the prisoner and then take a step back."

The warden turned to the condemned man and said, "This is the Walls Unit. We do things differently from the Ellis Unit, where you were being held. They have their way of doing things, and we have ours. We'll treat you as well as you allow us to treat you. If you act up, we'll act up, too; if you decide to be nice and civil, we'll be nice and treat you with respect. That's how it works. It's down to you how you're treated here."

The inmate nodded to let the warden know that he understood. The warden then said that they would keep him in the loop about what was happening with his appeal and reassured him that nothing would happen until a final court ruling had been made.

"He was very clear on that point—that we wouldn't accidentally kill him too soon."

The warden went through the same questions he always asked: whether the inmate had his affairs in order, whether he had made arrangements for what he wanted to happen with his body and possessions. He replied that everything was in order, and then the warden continued, "Do you have any questions for me?"

"You got any cigarettes?" the inmate asked.

Jim laughs.

"I can't tell you how many times I heard that. It was always the first question from the folks who were sentenced to death, and the warden never gave them a yes or a no. Instead, he said, 'We'll see what we can do.'"

The warden himself never handed over any cigarettes to the inmates, but he let Jim do it.

"I used to go and buy them a pack, but the warden always paid out of his own pocket. I worked under five different wardens over the years, and it was always the same: they gave me the money to buy cigarettes. Everything had its place in the routine, and it was all pretty strict, but they didn't want to make the situation any worse for the men. The simple truth is that the calmer the inmates were, the easier they were to deal with. So, they always got their cigarettes."

Once the warden had left, Jim gave the prisoner a cigarette and helped him to light it. The inmate then sat down on the bunk with his coffee.

Jim grabbed a chair and sat opposite him on the other side of the bars. He said they should get started and immediately confessed, "I'm terrified. This is my first execution."

"Mine too," the man replied.

They both smiled.

"I told him I had seen people die before and that I knew what to expect, but that I'd never spoken to anyone awaiting the death sentence like this and that I wanted him to know that anything he said would stay between us. After that, I said, 'When I feel anxious like I do right now, I put my faith and trust in Jesus. He is my peace and my hope. He is everything to me.'"

The inmate replied that that was where he found strength, too.

Jim stared at him in astonishment. "In Jesus?"

"Sure."

A confused Jim looked down at the papers in front of him before turning his attention back to the inmate.

"I don't understand. Your file says that you're Muslim."

The inmate smiled and said, "I'm not Muslim."

That was Jim's first lesson in what he calls "the prison game.

"Muslims have far more holy days, and they get extra privileges in terms of special food. There's a general belief that they're treated better than Christians, and that's the reason why many inmates—particularly African Americans —become Muslim. The truth is that Islam is the fastest-growing religion among the prison population. Still, I asked again whether we shared the same faith, and he told me he had grown up with Jesus."

As the afternoon wore on, the two men kept chatting, mostly small talk. At 3:00, the lawyer arrived to speak to his client, and Jim left the cell to make his way over the road to the Hospitality House, where the dying man's relatives were waiting.

"I remember they were very quiet to begin with."

The Hospitality House had been built by the Texas Baptist community to provide a place for the family and friends of the condemned to spend time in the lead-up to the execution.

"The man who built it was a kind, loving soul. I was very fond of him. He was actually an opponent of the death penalty, completely against it, but he had resigned himself to the fact that it existed. He wanted those families to have a place to gather, and he allowed us to go over and meet them."

Jim took the relatives through everything that would happen over the next few hours.

"They let me pray with them. I felt a sense of freedom with the inmate's family. I talked about Jesus' love and was able to speak from the heart."

· · ·

He returned to the death house just in time for the inmate's final meal, a cheeseburger and fries. Jim was served the same.

"Back then, the men could order whatever they liked from everything the prison had to offer. No one went out to get shrimp, steaks, or beer for them; they had to choose from what was available in the kitchen. Most of them just wanted cheeseburgers, anyway. And ice cream."

Going forward, once Jim had been at the prison a while and proved he was trustworthy, he was able to go out and collect any special food the inmates requested. But not on that day. For his first execution, everything went according to protocol.

They ate in silence and then got back to chatting. At around 6:00, the warden returned to the death house to let the inmate know that his appeal had been unsuccessful and that the execution was scheduled to take place at midnight.

"He wasn't surprised. He remained calm the whole time, solemn. We didn't have any trouble with him at all. When I heard the words 'Your appeal wasn't successful,' it actually came as a relief to me in my role as chaplain because I knew what I was up against."

Jim tells me that until the warden uttered those words, there was always a glimmer of hope. Until that moment, he didn't want to focus on the absolute certainty that the man was going to die. Instead, one part of him continued to think that there was a *chance* he would die. Once word came through, however, they both knew that the inmate's life really would end that evening, which meant a different aspect of his work could begin.

· · ·

Jim Brazzil explains that he often had to repeat the news to the prisoners, sometimes multiple times. It didn't really sink in for many of them. The inmate told me about his crime. He was convicted of murdering a seventy-five-year-old security guard during a robbery. He admitted it.

The hours passed, and a guard came by occasionally to check that everything was okay. The warden also visited several times, but for the most part, Jim and the prisoner were left alone.

The closer to the execution they came, the more uncomfortable the atmosphere grew. The man who had only hours left to live paced back and forth in his cell, smoking and pacing, smoking and pacing.

"I read to him from the Bible, and we listened to the radio. He had it on in the background. We chatted, too. I tried to make him understand that I knew where he was at. I don't know if I managed it, but I wanted to tell him all the same."

Around twenty minutes before midnight, activity in the death house really began to ramp up.

"You could hear people walking by behind his cell, heading into the chamber and through to the so-called drug room. That was where they prepared the chemicals for the execution. You could hear it all from his cell."

The condemned prisoners always grew tense at that point in the process. Going forward, Jim tried to prepare them for what they were about to hear before it started, but on that first occasion, he hadn't known what was coming.

As with all inmates facing execution, this inmate had been given a choice between wearing free-world clothes or a white prison jumpsuit.

"You have to understand the prison lingo. There are prisons, and then there's the free world. That's what we call it."

The inmate had chosen the white jumpsuit with DR, for Death Row, printed on the back. It was dazzlingly bright, starched, ironed, and ready and waiting for him on the bunk.

"As he got dressed, he said, 'Guess this is my death outfit.' I told him I understood why he saw it that way."

The chaplain was uneasy. Time was passing very quickly, and though the man claimed to have a good relationship with Jesus, Jim wasn't sure whether the man in front of him would really reach Heaven. He felt that if he didn't, he would have failed in his job.

Jim asked whether the prisoner would like to pray, and when he said yes, that did help.

"We prayed together, and he was calmer afterward. We talked about superficial things rather than what was about to happen—chit-chat. I told him the warden would come in and say, 'It's time' at any moment. Those words were the signal."

At two minutes past midnight, the prison warden did just that.

"It's time."

A group of guards—Jim doesn't remember whether there were seven or eight of them—were present, just in case the inmate put up a fight. But he didn't.

"We walked into the death chamber together, right over to the gurney. He hopped up himself, which was a huge relief to me. He then lay back, and they strapped him down."

The first team completed their tasks in roughly eight seconds and went on their way. At that point, another door opened, and the drug team came in—the needle boys, as Jim calls them.

"When they took out the needles, I got real nervous. I started talking to him non-stop in an attempt to distract him and let them do their job. They inserted an IV line into each arm and then wound bandages around both to secure them to the armrests. After that, we said another prayer."

Jim prayed for God to take care of the man and to give him peace.

"I remember I was by the foot of the gurney. The warden was by his head, and I was by his feet, and that's when they invited the witnesses into the room. Once they were all in place, the warden asked, 'Do you have anything you would like to say?'"

It isn't a right enshrined in law, but allowing those facing execution a final statement is a tradition older than the U.S. Constitution. When George Burroughs climbed the scaffold ahead of his own execution for witchcraft in 1692, he moved the crowd in Salem to tears with a perfect recitation of the Lord's Prayer before being hanged.

The inmate chose to speak. "I want the world to know that I'm innocent and that I've found peace. Let's ride."

Jim looked down at the man who had used his last words to protest his innocence—the same man who confessed his guilt to him just a few hours earlier.

"He didn't want to admit it to them, but he'd done it with me. That sort of thing happens pretty often."

The former chaplain falls silent for a moment, deep in thought.

"There are a couple of reasons why they might maintain

their innocence—their mom, their family. The inmates were always advised by their lawyers never to confess to anyone, which made it hard for them to tell the truth in the end after keeping that up for so long. But for me, it didn't feel right that the last thing he ever did was tell a lie. I always felt a huge void whenever that happened; I felt frustrated, upset, and resigned because so many of them had come so close to meeting death at peace, and yet they fell short. It would have made me respect him far more if he had just confessed."

Jim Brazzil says this is the first time he has ever talked to anyone about this.

"In a way, I guess I'm breaking his trust, but as the years go by, I can't help but think it would bring comfort to both the victim's family and his own if I told the truth about him and all the other inmates I met. Those relatives have waited so long. I just hope that anyone who needs that reads this book and learns the truth at last."

With that, Jim's very first execution finally got underway.

"I remember looking up at the little box on the wall and seeing that the liquid was already flowing down through both IV lines. His reaction came quickly, probably only a few seconds later. As the sodium pentothal, the sedative, started to work, I remember taking a deep breath as he struggled to breathe. He gasped for air at least four or five times, and then I saw them inject the second substance, the pancuronium bromide, to stop his breathing. He took his last breath then. Seeing a person's final breath was always a profound moment for me."

Jim closes his eyes and pauses.

"The last breath means it's all over—knowing that he's

dead—that no one will ever talk to him again, and I was the last person to really speak with him. It almost feels like a moment for reverence because God is right there in that room. I felt that."

The inmate may have stopped breathing, but his heart kept beating.

"You could see it on his chest and by his collar. I remember focusing on his collar the whole time. You could really see his heart pounding. But once they injected the potassium chloride, it gradually slowed. That's when you know it's truly over. And from the moment when his heart stopped beating, we waited four minutes."

Medically speaking, there are two types of death on death row: clinical death and biological death. Clinical death occurs when a person stops breathing, and their heart stops beating. After four minutes without oxygen, a body is considered to be irreversibly or biologically dead.

"They waited four minutes, and those four minutes felt like an eternity. There was complete silence. The room felt empty, aside from the man lying on the gurney. The warden was standing with his hands clasped in front of him, and no one moved a muscle. It was so quiet."

Right there and then, Jim felt a sudden jolt of fear.

"Did I do the right thing? Knowing that this man had died and was no longer a part of our world, that he now stood before God on the day of his judgment... I remember praying for him after he passed, asking God to receive him and show him mercy."

After four minutes, the prison warden, who was in

charge of everything that happened in the chamber, opened the door and brought in the doctor.

Dr. Wells didn't fit the stereotypical image of a medical doctor.

"He had a big, bushy beard that extended right down to his throat. The man was a farmer, but he was also a doctor in the E.R. and had an office in town. He was a bit of a renegade, the kind of person who does what he wants, but whenever he came into the death chamber, he always did things the same way. He wore a stethoscope around his neck and would nod quickly to show his respect before he got to work checking for a pulse. He tried both sides of the prisoner's neck and then shone a little flashlight in his eyes. After that, he put the flashlight down and listened for a pulse with his stethoscope before finally calling the time. The prison warden always repeated that because it became the official time of death."

Jim doesn't remember the exact time that day, but he does know that it was late, that he didn't leave the prison until 2:30 in the morning.

"The inmate's family hadn't claimed the body, so the warden turned to me and said, 'I need you back here at eight. We'll have to bury him.' I was exhausted, but I had so many thoughts."

At that point in time, all of Jim's furniture was in his new apartment in Gatesville, almost three hours away. As a result, he was sleeping in the garage of a retired local priest.

"His name was Emmett Solomon, a devout man. I really loved him. I wanted to go inside and wake him up so we could talk through everything, but I didn't. I remember just going out to the garage, lying down, breathing in the gas fumes, and not having anyone to talk to. I was worked up and exhausted. It was such a powerful moment. To me, it hadn't been an execution; it was a religious experience. Knowing that this man had come into the presence of God. Whether or not he was accepted wasn't my decision."

Despite his final lie, Jim believes the inmate reached Heaven that night.

"Because that's the promise God makes to us. If we take Jesus as our savior, we will be welcomed into Heaven. He said, 'I forgive you your sins and allow you into Heaven.' The prisoner looked so peaceful as he died, and he had opened his heart to Jesus, so that's what I choose to believe. You could call it the Brazzil interpretation of the Bible."

The chaplain slept badly that night.

"It was one of those nights you spend half-awake, tossing and turning. But I did make it to work the next morning, and I'd changed my clothes like I was told into a blue sports jacket, a tie, black pants, black shoes, and a black belt. I was tired, and the warden had just arrived. He was tired and grumpy, too, but he nodded to me and said, 'Well, let's go bury him.'"

They got to Joe Byrd Cemetery just after 8:30, right as the funeral director arrived with the coffin. A few of the inmates had prepared everything at the graveside and had already placed the casket-lowering device.

"We lifted the coffin onto it, and I got ready to begin the service. It was my first visit to the cemetery."

He found it to be an unusually sad place.

"Probably because there were so many graves there. I

didn't know why it was named after Joe Byrd at the time; I didn't know anything about it. I just looked out at the rows of headstones and crosses. The paint had flaked on some of them, making it almost impossible to read the names, and others had no text at all. Just think about that, about your life being so meaningless that you end up with a blank cross on your grave."

The chaplain and the warden approached the casket. None of the inmate's relatives were in attendance that day. They were the only two present.

The prison warden went off to talk to a couple of laborers, leaving Jim alone with the coffin. He noticed that nothing but a small hook held the lid shut, so he opened it.

"I don't know why I wanted to see what was inside. I guess it was because... I had a lot of things I needed to process. He was all blotchy. Purple and red. His face was so blotchy."

That was how Jim learned that when a person is executed... when they are starved of oxygen, their face turns a deep shade of purple. After some time, patches of everything from lilac to pink can also appear.

"So many different shades, all over him. I reached out and touched his hand. It was only six hours since he died, so it wasn't too cold."

For some reason, Jim found the fact that he was burying a man so soon after death deeply moving.

"Six hours after he died, he was six feet under. I was the last person to talk to him. The last person to really see him. I stood there for a long time, just looking down at his dead body, until eventually, I heard the warden tell me to get started. So I shut the lid and began the funeral."

. . .

44

The gravediggers, fellow inmates from the Walls Unit, stood respectfully to one side, listening to the chaplain's words.

"I tried to make every funeral special. I never used the same old speech; I wanted it to reflect the individual. I used 'Let not your heart be troubled' from John 14:1-6. I remember speaking to the inmates present about the promise of hope after death, saying that without that hope, we would be sad and despondent. I also said that the person we were burying was a Christian and that he had told me so, even if he failed to mention it in his last words."

Jim told those gathered that God had welcomed the inmate into His kingdom.

"Funerals are for the living, not the dead. A person can't hear us once they pass, so a big part of a funeral is to bring comfort to those present. Saying the right thing can sow the seed of an idea and make people feel like they want that hope, that they want to reach God's kingdom one day. I've met multiple people who have welcomed Christ into their lives following a funeral."

Once the service was over, Jim said one last "Amen" before stepping back to allow the inmates to get on with their work. They lowered the coffin into the grave and began covering it with earth. The warden made his way back over to the car, but Jim held back.

"I guess it was my attempt to get some sort of closure. I saw him die, I saw him in the coffin, and I saw him being lowered into the ground. I also needed to see him disappear for good to really feel like it was all over. I remember walking away with the sense that his was a wasted life. And not just one, but two—

both the victim's and the executed man's. In all my work with death row prisoners, I quickly came to the conclusion that there are no winners as far as the death penalty is concerned.

"The death penalty doesn't satisfy anyone. Death is just a great separator. Nothing can bring the killer's victims back to life. Of course, the victim's relatives might feel a certain satisfaction in seeing him die, but they don't stand to gain anything else. I must have heard ten or eleven relatives say, 'Well, at least he can't hurt anyone else now, and that means I can rest easy.' But the whole process hurts them because it forces them to re-live their pain. It hurts the condemned man's relatives, too. And it was hard for the people who had to carry it out. No, when it comes to death, there are no winners. But I also realized early on that I couldn't allow myself to worry about whether the death penalty was right or wrong. It made no difference. The death penalty exists, and these people need Jesus. As their chaplain, I wanted to be able to talk to them during their last few hours, and so that's what I did."

If it was down to you, would Texas have the death penalty?

Jim Brazzil hesitates before he answers. He shifts slightly on the sofa.

"I'm really torn on the issue. I'm not an opponent of the death penalty, but I'm not an advocate of it either."

But what if you had the power? If someone turned to you and said, "Jim, if you say, 'yes' tomorrow, we'll put a stop to all executions in Texas."?

"I'd rather have the power to say, 'Don't kill anybody.'"

That's not an option.

"Why not?"

Because that's just wishful thinking. You can't stop people from killing one another. But the existence of the death penalty is something that can actually change.

"I guess I'd keep it, then."

You'd keep it?

"I would keep it."

Why?

"Just the knowledge of the crimes they've committed and their mentality. We don't... It might look like we're doing a horrible thing, but I can tell you that of the 155 prisoners I followed into the execution chamber, the overwhelming majority said, 'You're doing me a favor today. I can't imagine living the rest of my life in a small, cramped cell with no A/C while my mom has to travel back and forth and my family has to keep putting money into my account. You're not hurting me; you're setting me free.' I heard it so, so, so many times, and if it were down to me—if I were on death row—I would rather be executed than locked in that cell."

He tells me that Karla Faye Tucker, one of the most high-profile inmates he met on death row, said something along those lines.

"She said, 'Send me home. I know where I'm going. Don't give me a stay. If they give me a stay, don't tell me. Don't let them do it.'"

What did you do after they filled in that first inmate's grave?

"I walked back to the car, got in beside the warden, and let out a deep sigh."

The warden acknowledged his feelings by saying, "Pretty tough, huh?" Jim agreed that it was, and the warden said that he would love to give him the rest of the day off but that the tragic thing about executions was that they didn't cancel out everything else that needed doing around the prison; they just added extra work.

Jim nodded, and they drove back to the Walls Unit, where the morning had just begun.

As luck would have it, Jim's assistant Lisa had been around for countless executions during the previous chaplain's tenure, and she was waiting with a mug of coffee and a few minutes' chat when he got to the office. After that, it was back to business as usual.

"The inmates started dropping in to see me, and things got real busy. There was no time to think about anything else. We were run off our feet."

Later that day, the phone rang, and the prison warden asked Jim to come to his office.

"He said that everyone was pleased with my work and that he wanted me to consider staying in Huntsville to become the chaplain on death row. He added that I would be given a place to live and that he had already discussed the idea with his superiors."

Jim replied that he needed time to think. The whole reason for moving to Gatesville and taking a new job there was so that he could be closer to his family. But at the same time, he knew this was his calling.

The prison warden told him to take three days' vacation to think it through.

"I set off later that same evening. First, I drove to my wife's place to talk it over with her. I said, 'The whole reason for moving to Gatesville was to be closer to y'all. Maybe we could make a fresh start there.' But she told me she didn't want to start over, that nothing had changed. After that, I drove over to my mom's. I told her about the job offer, and she said, 'Jim if you move to Gatesville for my sake, you're doing it for the wrong reasons. This is your mission. You've got to do what God tells you to do.'"

Jim drove back to the garage in Huntsville, sat down, and prayed. He stayed there for the next two days until God had answered.

"I went back to the prison warden and said I would take the job."

He had spent his entire life searching, but Jim had finally found where he belonged—where God had told him to be.

"All my life, I felt inferior to everyone else. Mediocre."

He says this matter-of-factly, not as a complaint.

"I was mediocre when I finished high school, and I was mediocre when I graduated from college. I left the seminary a mediocre minister, and I wound up at a church—an ordinary, unremarkable church—and I failed there. And then there was my marriage. I had the opportunity to build a fantastic relationship with my wife, but I blew it. I was a mediocre husband, if that."

He shakes his head.

"When I first started working in prisons, I did it because I really did feel a calling. But it took two years before anyone actually hired me because I was mediocre. After a long time of not having done things right, I was finally in a place where I knew I could give one hundred percent. And I did. For the first time in my life, as a chaplain on death row, I was no longer mediocre."

Chapter Three

I remember thinking that everyone knew just how poor we were.

1941-1956

Jim Brazzil's father was Thomas Chester Brazzil, but everyone knew him as Chuck. Chuck was a simple soul. A dyed-in-the-wool redneck from the small community of Flat, roughly halfway between Dallas and Austin. He was an uneducated family man who always had a cigarette on the go and smelled like smoke and Old Spice. But he was also someone who had the ability to make whoever he was talking to feel like the only person in the room.

During World War II, Chuck enlisted on the same day as his two brothers, JD and Jim, and was sent to the Pacific.

"Jim, Dad's older brother, joined the Army as a war correspondent, but I don't know where he was sent. My old man was deployed to Hawaii, Australia, and the areas round about there. JD, his younger brother, too. He served on a destroyer; my dad was on the destroyer tender that sailed back and forth to supply it with whatever it needed. One day, Dad saw his brother's ship get hit by a torpedo and partially sink, and all he could do was watch. It took three days before they came up alongside JD's destroyer and he could go across to look for his brother. He expected to find him splattered up the wall or something, but fortunately, he managed to track him down pretty quickly, and he was completely unharmed."

Both brothers went home on leave in 1944, and their sister, who was training to become a nurse, invited a friend over to join the celebration. Martha Astenia Bratcher was nine years younger than Chuck, and according to her father, she was much too good for him.

"My mother was a city girl. She grew up in the Garland area, one of the better suburbs in the northeastern part of Dallas. They had someone who cleaned the house for them, so they must have been pretty wealthy. Her father was a successful guy. He was also an alcoholic who was cruel to his wife, but they didn't fight in front of the kids, for the most part, anyway."

Chuck Brazzil didn't see eye to eye with Martha's father.

"One day, Dad got into his old Ford Model A and drove from Flat to Dallas. When he got to her house, he knocked on the door. Her father came out, and they talked. I don't know what was said, but the conversation ended with her father telling Dad he could marry her. Mom packed her bag and left that same evening. They went to Gatesville the very next day, applied for their marriage license, and got married. Her family wasn't there, and neither was his. It was just the two of them."

This was in November 1945. Their first son, Thomas Earl Brazzil, was born two years later, on June 10th, 1947. Then, on March 19th, 1950, James Ferrell Brazzil arrived—or Jim, as he has always been known.

"Mom had a miscarriage between Tom and me, and that crushed her. Dad said she had an emotional breakdown, whatever that meant at the time. That's all I really know. They never talked about it."

For the first few years of Jim's life, the family struggled to make a living off a 200-acre farm that his grandfather owned. But the old place was really nothing but flint rocks and cedar trees. Chuck then tried his luck in Fort Worth, working on the B-36 airplanes. But there was no longer a demand since the war was over. Chuck then got a job in Temple, working for the Texas Highway Department. While on the job, he was riding in the back of a dump truck. The driver turned too fast, and all the men in the back fell out. Jim's dad was hospitalized for weeks, but his leg never healed correctly. Finally, the family moved back to Flat to live in an old friend's house. The family had no money, and their home in Flat was—in Jim's own words—a dump. Four rooms, no toilet, no running water. Still, they lived there rent-free, and there was a wood-burning stove in the middle of the house, which kept it reasonably warm.

"When the wind blew, the wallpaper came loose from the walls. It was a tough life, it really was."

Their meals revolved around beans, potatoes, and cornbread, and for the most part, they did without meat. The only time they enjoyed that luxury was when Jim, Tom, or their father had been out with the .410 shotgun that was kept under Jim's bed. On days like that, the good days, they might eat rabbit, squirrel, or venison for dinner.

The way the family celebrated Christmas hinged on the number of pecans they had managed to gather that fall. There were around a hundred pecan trees by the creek near their house, and Jim and his brother would go down there every day.

"Back then, you could walk right across other people's property; they didn't care. We'd take a big stick and knock the pecans down from the trees. There was a place that shelled them not far from where we lived, so Dad would take them over there and sell them. I don't know how much money that brought in, but it paid for our Christmas gifts. How good they were depended on how many nuts we brought home."

From an early age, Jim learned never to ask for anything because his family simply couldn't afford it, but his father always gave him something special at Christmas.

"I got a Fort Apache fort one year, and that was a dream come true. In the following years, I got a BB gun and a fishing rod. None of the gifts were expensive, but to me, they were fantastic."

The family eventually left their hovel and moved to a better house, still in the poorer area on the east side of town. Jim also joined the Cub Scouts.

He gets up from the sofa and fetches a photograph of

himself as a young boy dressed up in his scout uniform. His little face is beaming.

"One of the highlights of my life was becoming a scout. I liked going there so much; I really did. Once, I think it must've been two or three days before Christmas, I heard a knock at the door. I went to answer it, and it was my Cub Scout pack."

The boys were all clutching toys and food, and they carried everything inside.

"I remember how it felt to see them march into our house with all the food and gifts and realize they knew I was poor and didn't have a thing. That's when it really hit me just how poor we were."

One of the gifts contained the very thing he had been hoping for that year: a bow and arrow.

"I wanted to be happy about it, but I was so ashamed that they had seen our poverty. I moved up to the Boy Scouts not long after, and the same thing happened with my new troop the very next Christmas."

A year after that, there was another knock at the door. This time, members of the local congregation delivered food and gifts to the poorest families in the area.

"I remember thinking that everyone knew just how poor we were. I know their hearts were in the right place, but whenever I saw my friends after that, I got the sense they were looking at me differently. That's a feeling I've carried with me ever since."

Jim was often sick as a child, really sick, and the problems started before his first birthday.

"I had serious issues with my ears. My eardrums would

burst pretty much every month, and I'd have blood and puss coming out of my ears. When I was in first grade, they removed my tonsils in the hopes that it would help, but it didn't make any difference. The doctor said there was nothing he could do and that I needed to see a specialist, so they took me to the Scott & White Hospital and performed a so-called mastoidectomy. That involved making an incision behind my ear and pushing it forward. They then cleaned up the Mastoid bone and removed part of it."

He smiles at the macabre memory.

"They literally made a cut and just peeled my ear forward and laid it on the side of my head."

It was quickly realized that Jim had a serious, ongoing problem with his ear.

"But we couldn't afford to keep going to the doctor. Whenever I got an earache, Mom would cook up some corn-meal and wrap it in a towel that she'd press to my ear. That was my very own heat pad, and it always helped a little. Even so, I'd be in pain for hours and hours. I sat there with my feet on a stool and the cornmeal on the side of my head, pain pulsing through my ear. All I could think about was the pain. I felt so helpless, and then suddenly, my eardrum would burst, and all this gunk would come flooding out. It was always such a relief when that happened. I can't describe how good it felt after being in such pain."

Jim's aunt was a surgical nurse in the Army. When he was ten, she arranged for him to see a military ear specialist free of charge. He was a friend of hers.

"It was a Sunday afternoon when we went over to the veterans' hospital in Temple to the clinical unit. Strictly speaking, they were supposed to be closed on Sundays, but I met a tall man, a giant of a doctor with a mustache. He sat me down, examined my ears, and said, 'Young man, do you think you could stay here while I talk to your mom and dad in the next room?' I did as he asked, but I still heard every word they said in there."

The doctor told Jim's parents that their son had a severe ear infection that had spread to the bone. If it managed to cross the skull and reach his brain, it would kill him.

Jim can still remember the doctor's final words that day, "As things stand, I don't think he'll live to see his twelfth birthday."

His ten-year-old self was terrified.

"I didn't tell them I knew; I didn't want them to worry. But that was when I realized that my relationship with God would be so important. I really did think I would die before I turned twelve. Fortunately, the infection never reached my brain. It didn't go away; it just stopped spreading. I still have it to this day."

From that moment on, death was always at the back of Jim's mind.

"The fact that I might die... When you're ten, you're supposed to think about all the exciting things to come, things people always ask about. You know, like, 'What do you want to be when you grow up?' But I didn't know what I wanted to be because I'd found out I wouldn't be alive. I couldn't see a future for myself. That's supposed to be one of the best times of a kid's life, but it was the worst year of mine."

I flinch slightly, but I don't think he has noticed. He has, of course. I've started to realize that few things escape Jim.

"Did something happen when you were ten?"

I think it was the worst year of my life, too.

"Why?"

I'm the one interviewing you, not the other way around. Besides, it wasn't a death sentence, so you win.

"It's not a competition. I'm happy to listen."

I'm happy to listen. Those words—I wonder how many times he has said them to someone facing death. I'm happy to listen. I wonder whether those men and women found it as easy to open up to him as I do.

I tell him that I was ten when my parents got divorced. My dad leaned across the table one day and spat in my mother's face. She got up, walked out, and never came back. My older brother and I were left behind... with him.

I tell him that Dad got angrier and angrier when he found out she had met someone else. He sat at the kitchen table and painted the most awful pictures of her—of what she was doing and how she sounded. My brother and I sat there with our breakfast, desperately wishing he would stop talking.

That he never stopped talking.

I tell Jim about the car rides that lasted for hours as he drove round and round, talking about how much better the world would be without her. And that, one evening when he was particularly worked up, he told us that her shift finished at midnight. He said it perfectly matter of fact.

Jim sits quietly as I recount how I ran into the kitchen in a blind panic. I opened the first drawer I came to and fumbled for something I could use to defend her, convinced she was going to die that night. I grabbed an ordinary table knife and ran outside to hide beneath the big oak and wait.

I tell him that I stared down at the sea of blue scilla beneath my feet and that, for some reason, it felt comforting to have them keep me company. I still can't see those flowers without remembering that night. I heard footsteps approaching and ran forward, clutching the knife, startling my mother. I tell him that she ushered me into the house and made me tell her what had happened.

Ten wasn't a good age for me either.

Jim nods and waits for me to go on in case there is anything else I want to say. I share a few more memories; they just come flooding out—events which, for legal reasons, I can't get into here. My father has never been convicted of any crime.

It's so easy to talk to Jim, but I feel guilty every time I interrupt his story with mine. We're here because he has a story to tell, not the other way around. And yet, with every word I say, the ever-present weight on my chest seems to get a little lighter. I wonder if this was how the inmates felt after spending time with him.

After receiving his death sentence, Jim realized that his days were probably numbered and that he should use the time he had left as wisely as possible. Since then, Jim Brazzil has heard God's voice in everything he does. He has listened carefully and paid close attention.

"I guess it made me appreciate what I had in a very special way. I don't know how else to explain it. I started enjoying everything. I really wanted to live. I remember paying more attention to nature. I might sit under one of the trees—there was a grove of cedar trees nearby—and spend hours there. That's not something most ten or eleven-year-olds would do, but I just enjoyed spending time with God, praying, and soaking up the beauty. Thanking Him for what I saw. It really brought me closer to God in a very real sense."

He tells me that his desire to experience things quickly expanded to include girls but that the opposite sex remained a mystery to him.

"I never did anything other than kiss my girlfriends. I respected them and didn't want to force myself onto them. I just wanted it to be... It didn't feel right to have sex outside of marriage. I wanted to wait until I had a wife."

I ask him whether he ended up saving himself for marriage.

Jim Brazzil looks down.

"No."

Chapter Four

I knew in my heart that I wanted to serve God,
but I also had so much desire within me.

1966-1967

When he was sixteen, Jim took part in a church camp in Austin. A visiting missionary from Zambia delivered a sermon, and his words were so moving that Jim forgot to take notes like he usually did. All he could do was listen as the man spoke about devoting his life to Christ—not just living with God but *serving* Him.

"Going out and preaching the gospel, heading out into the world as a missionary. He quoted straight from Isaiah, chapter 6, where God asks: 'Whom shall I send, and who will go for us?' and Isiah says, 'I, here am I; send me.' I can still remember the tabernacle. It was huge, with space for at least 500 kids, and it was hot and stuffy. After the sermon, I remember lying on my bed and feeling God's presence. I couldn't *hear* anything but felt like God was talking to me."

Jim spent a long time thinking about it afterward, grappling with the idea. But in the end, in November of that year, he told his parents that he was struggling with becoming a pastor. His father replied that it was between him and God, which wasn't much help. Jim waited another two months, until January 1967, before reaching out to his own pastor and explaining that God had called upon him to preach.

"It was frightening because I knew in my heart that I wanted to serve God, but I also had so much desire within me. I had a longing for sex and to be a part of the world and live life to the fullest. The idea that I would have to give any of that up was difficult. Would it be worth it? Would I be able to do it? Would people listen to me? I had so many doubts. But then, one day, I realized I was mature enough to say, 'Yeah, I'm going to do it.' I walked up to the front of the church and said that I wanted to give myself over to becoming a pastor in the congregation and let God use me as He wished."

That was March 19, 1967. Jim's seventeenth birthday. A Sunday.

"I just knew. It hit me like a lightning bolt. I don't know how else to explain it. The feeling was even stronger than the day when I accepted Jesus as my savior, probably because I was older. It was more definitive, more direct. I knew it would have lasting consequences."

The Baptist church to which he belonged voted to award

Jim Brazzil a pastor's license, which he still has to this day. In the state of Texas, that license allowed him to conduct marriages and funerals and preach, though not to perform communion or baptisms. For that, a person has to be ordinated.

Around two months later, on May 12—Mother's Day—Jim gave his first sermon.

"My mom was there, and my dad and brother, too. The church was actually full that evening. I had family members from both of my parents' sides travel to hear that first sermon."

The Master Needs Men was the title.

"I remember I talked about Moses. About Noah. Under difficult circumstances, God called on Noah to save a handful of people who would change the world. They built the Ark, and that was the image I conjured up that day. But I was so nervous that I managed to put Moses in the Ark instead of Noah. Afterward, Mom was the first person who came over to me. She didn't say 'great job' or 'that was beautiful' or anything like that. She said, 'You put Moses in the Ark and Nicodemus in the tree.' Talk about bringing me back down to earth."

Jim felt awful, like an utter failure, and he was unsure of himself yet again.

"I went through the whole spectrum of emotions. I knew I wanted to be a minister, and I had already promised to preach God's word, but in a way, I was actually rebelling against that. I was seventeen. I knew it would mean I couldn't do any of the things my friends were doing, like partying, drinking beer, having a bunch of sex, and trying drugs—which were everywhere at the time—because that would be devastating to my role as God's witness. I was torn."

Jim joined two friends for coffee one evening around this time. One was his age, the other a couple of years older.

"My buddy, who was the same age as me, said he really needed a woman, and the older guy said he had a car and that it could be arranged."

Jim told them he didn't have any money, but the older of the two said not to worry.

They drove to a place called the Chicken Ranch in Fayette County, around three miles east of central La Grange. Between 1905 and 1973, the Chicken Ranch was an illegal brothel. It rose to fame in the early 1980s as a result of the musical comedy *The Best Little Whorehouse in Texas,* starring Dolly Parton and Burt Reynolds. One of the tracks Dolly Parton recorded for the film was 'I Will Always Love You,' though this time, it was about fleeting lust rather than never-ending love.

It cost Jim twenty dollars to lose his virginity at the best little whorehouse in Texas.

"Her name was Kim, and she was a college student. She taught me what to do. I could have gotten a cheaper rate, but she said, 'This is your first time, why not go around the world? That'll be twenty dollars.' I had a twenty dollar bill in my pocket, so I gave it to her."

Jim looks uncomfortable, but he goes on.

"First, she pulled my pants down to check that everything looked okay. I almost climaxed right there and then, just from her eyes on me. She got me cleaned up, and then she let me try out any position I wanted. That was what she meant by 'around the world.' Whatever I felt like doing."

He is quiet for a few seconds.

"I felt terrible. I mean, it was wonderful, but I also felt like I'd betrayed God—like I'd betrayed myself. I had given my virginity away, and I felt awful about it—so awful that I decided I wouldn't do anything like that again until I met the woman I wanted to marry. And that was that."

How do you feel about it now, talking about what happened all these years later? About losing your virginity to a prostitute in Le Grange?

"I never thought of her as a prostitute; I didn't. Even though that's exactly what she was. Kim was pretty—blonde-haired, blue-eyed, in her mid-twenties. Much older than me, in other words. I was only seventeen. She was so experienced and so tender, too. She was... how can I put it...? There was nothing crude or sleazy about it; there really wasn't—nothing ugly. It was a beautiful experience. In some ways, I regret not saving myself, but in others, it makes me smile. Does that make sense?"

Our feelings are often contradictory. I have to admit that I'm conflicted over what you just said. I'm a little surprised.

. . .

"Back then, I didn't know anything about girls. They were so elusive to me. I didn't understand them. All I knew was that they were precious and delicate and that I didn't want to hurt them."

Nowadays, many people consider buying sex to be a form of abuse.

"I could never have forced myself onto anyone. Nothing would have happened if I knew someone wasn't interested in me."

Though, if you're buying sex from a person, they aren't interested in you.

"No, and I understand that now. I think that if I'd gotten my way when I was younger, I would have had a lot more sex. I liked it. I still do, though I can't claim to do it so often these days. It's not so easy when you have prostate cancer, and I know there'll be less and less of it with each year that passes."

He sighs, visibly uncomfortable.

"I wouldn't say I had the easiest of lives. I've always been aware of my poverty, and I've never forgotten that. A little later, as I got older, I really did feel unworthy. If I was interested in a girl while I was in school, I always told myself that I wasn't good enough for her because I was ugly and didn't have any money. I had nothing to offer them. But the older I get, the more valuable women become to me. I feel that they need to be treated with care, dignity, and respect. I'm deeply grateful for my wife now—for all women. I believe they deserve so much more than men can give them. I would be nothing without my wife. Today, I would never be able to use a woman purely to satisfy my own sexual needs, but that's what I did with Kim, and I'm sure I did it with my first wife, too."

Chapter Five

You have to be able to live with yourself.
That's universal. Whether you believe in God or not.

1967-1973

After his visit to the brothel, Jim stopped preaching.

"I spent months feeling ashamed. I did nothing but pray, and once I knew that God had forgiven me, it was much easier to forgive myself."

How does a person forgive themselves?

"By praying. By praying non-stop."

. . .

What if it's not as easy as simply offloading it onto God? If, unlike you, a person doesn't have God in their life but still needs to forgive themselves?

"You have to be able to live with yourself. That's universal. Whether you believe in God or not. I've met plenty of inmates who didn't want God in their lives, but it's about reaching a point where you can accept the things you've done and feel like you don't want to do them again. A person can have Christian morals and values without actually being a Christian. It's still possible to find peace. Not the sort of peace I would wish on people, but peace all the same."

Jim eventually enrolled at a small Baptist college in Brownwood, Texas.

"Howard Payne was a private school, which meant it was extremely expensive, but they ran a special program at the time, the guaranteed tuition program. It meant I could take as many classes as I wanted for a fixed fee. It cost me 399 dollars a semester. The year I joined was the last year they offered that deal, but because I'd enrolled on those terms, I was allowed to continue paying the same amount for as long as I studied there. I worked two jobs just to make ends meet: doing maintenance on campus and as a janitor at the church back home on weekends. All in all, I managed to complete my studies in three and a half years. I rushed through the program as quickly as I could because I knew I couldn't afford to stay for any longer than that. It was really hard work, but I graduated with a major in Bible Studies and minors in Greek and History."

. . .

Toward the end of Jim's sophomore year, his pastor said they needed to talk. He told Jim about a small Baptist church in the community of Belton, less than 30 miles southwest. It had been having a rough time and was on the verge of having to close its doors. The congregation had rallied around, but they had been without a pastor for over a year and wouldn't be able to last much longer.

Jim said he would be happy to give a sermon there, but the pastor replied that sermons weren't what the congregation needed.

"They need someone who will love them. They need a pastor."

Jim said no—that he wasn't ready and hadn't even finished his studies yet. However, the pastor said that he didn't need a degree in order to love people, be a shepherd to them, and help them grow. They agreed that Jim would go over and preach to them one Sunday and that they would take it from there.

Seven members of the congregation turned out that day.

"Almost all of them were older, though there was also a teenage girl who was learning to play piano."

The church didn't have its own cantor, just an old lady who played the piano and missed every other note.

"It was terrible. The church had one deacon, and he was also the choirmaster. He'd had one lung removed due to lung cancer, so whenever he sang, it just sounded like 'Uhhhh.' I fell in love with them pretty much right away. They were so sweet and supportive and asked me to come back the next week."

Those seven people were present for Jim's second

sermon in Belton. For six weeks in a row, in fact, he preached to the same handful of faces. But on the seventh week, there were two new congregants. Jim invited two of his friends to come and play southern gospel music in the church, and after that, things exploded.

"It was a lot of fun to see so many people come to Jesus."

They asked him to become their pastor, and at just nineteen years of age, he said yes. The job paid $18.50 a week, and he continued working as a maintenance worker on campus and attending more classes than he had time for. Jim's grades weren't especially good, though he passed almost every subject—everything except second-year English. He had taken it as a summer course, but after coming down with a bout of the flu, he had to drop out. He didn't think it mattered that he never got around to re-taking it.

Throughout his time at college, Jim stayed away from girls.

"I still didn't think I deserved to be with any of them. I was broke. I had no money and nothing to offer. My health was poor, and I was constantly having to go to the doctor. I wasn't good-looking, and I wasn't especially masculine; I was small and thin. So I just forgot all about that part of life."

In the spring of 1970, roller skating became popular in the United States. The activity had been in vogue for some time, but it wasn't until the early seventies that it hit new heights thanks to the rise of disco music. There were many roller-skating rinks in Texas, and Jim was a big fan. He attended his local every single week, and he knew almost everyone there.

One day, however, he spotted a young woman he had never seen before.

"She was really short, with thick, dark brown hair. Very cute. She was also alone. I asked if she would like to join me, and we started skating together."

Her name was Janice, and she was a student at First Baptist Church Academy. Jim was thrilled to discover that she was Christian. She was seventeen at the time, Jim twenty.

Janice told him that the younger members of her church were planning to go bowling the next evening and that he was welcome to join them. Jim thought that sounded fun, so he turned up at the alley the next evening and spent the whole time talking to Janice and her pastor. Three weeks later, Jim decided to throw a party at the little church in Belton. The only problem was that there were almost no young members of the congregation, so he got in touch with Janice and asked whether she and a few of her friends might be willing to join them in the hopes of tempting a few more locals to come along.

Janice replied that she would love to.

"One of my buddies had a forty-foot flatbed trailer, and he brought it over and covered it in hay. We filled the trailer with young people, and that party was the turning point for the church. It was great in every sense of the word. I kissed Janice and asked if she would like to be my girlfriend that evening, and she said yes. That was the start of our relationship."

This was August 1970.

"I gave her a ring in December, around Christmastime. I knew I was going to propose. I'd already told Mom and Dad one evening when I went home to visit on a Friday. They said, 'We thought you might. We can see how much you care about her.' They gave me their blessing, and I actually took Mom with me to buy the ring."

Jim proposed in his 1965 Pontiac Catalina. It was the kind of car with bench seats in the front and back, a great big thing that didn't do much more than ten miles a gallon.

"I turned to her in the car that evening and said, 'I've done a lot of praying about this, Janice, and I was wondering if you would consider being my wife.' She said she would, and so I gave her the ring. It was wonderful. A dream come true. There was a beautiful full moon above us that night. It really was fabulous."

One year later, the couple got married at East Side Baptist, the church he had attended growing up. Unfortunately for Jim, the marital bliss he had hoped for failed to materialize.

"We were bad at communicating with each other, so there was a lot of frustration there."

Jim was about to graduate at the time, but two weeks before the ceremony, he received a letter from his college. A final review of his grades revealed that he never completed second-year English, which meant he couldn't receive his diploma.

"When we got married, I had sixty-five dollars to my name. I had a Pontiac Catalina and a wife but no college degree. We rented a tiny apartment that cost eighty-five dollars a month, and I couldn't even afford the first install-ment. I had no intention of returning to Brownwood to keep studying now that I had a wife and a place to live, but I didn't know what else to do. I still had the job at the church in Belton, so I thought I'd stay there and try to save a little money. I managed to find extra work as a house painter, and I did that for a few weeks."

Not long later, he saw an advertisement for a job in the engineering department of the Texas Highway Department, where his father and brother already worked.

"I submitted an application. Twenty-two people were hoping to get the job, but I'd taken a geology class in college. None of the others had even attended university, so those geology classes gave me the edge. I started working in the lab at the Highway Department."

Janice also took up a post as a clerk at Scott & White Hospital to help bolster their finances.

"We got married in December '71, so this must have been 1972. I didn't have enough money to return to school that spring, so I missed an entire year. It wasn't until the spring of 1973 that I enrolled at Temple Junior College to take sophomore English. I did evening classes after the working day was over, three hours every night. I took that course and hated every minute of it; I thought it was such a waste of my time."

But in May 1973, Jim finally got his college diploma. The future looked brighter than it had in a long time, especially since Janice was six months pregnant with their first child, Misty.

Chapter Six

*I wanted to give her a glimmer of hope,
even though the situation was hopeless.*

1974-1980

The growing family moved to Bertram, around forty miles
outside of Austin. Misty was almost a year old, and Jim had
found a new job as a pastor in the small community of under
800 inhabitants.

"Bertram holds a special place in my heart. I loved it
then, and I love it now, but so many things happened there.
It was in Bertram that I first saw someone die."

Rural Texas had very little ambulance coverage at the
time, so Jim and a few neighbors started a voluntary organization providing first aid in emergencies. They didn't have

an ambulance, but the community did have a rapid response vehicle.

One cold night, Jim responded to an emergency call. He and a colleague drove out to the site of an accident on the outskirts of the city, along the long, winding road toward Marble Falls. Two cars had crashed head-on on a bend, and the driver of one of them was already dead.

"He was my first. I have to say it felt spiritual somehow. I was completely switched off, but I still took it all in. It was like I could see myself standing there, but I didn't allow myself to get emotional. You can't when you have a job to do, though I knew I would have to process it at some point. As I stood there looking at him, I remember thinking, 'I wonder if he's in Heaven now?'"

Jim checked the man for signs of life. They were forty-five minutes from the nearest ambulance, and he couldn't feel a pulse, so he didn't attempt CPR.

During our first interview, you said that no one should have to die alone. Is this when you realized that?

"Around that time, a little later."

Jim and his colleague received another call about a head-on collision on the busy highway cutting through the small community of Briggs.

"I won't get into the gory details, but when we arrived at the scene, we found a woman trapped in one of the cars. The driver of the second vehicle was already dead. I remember climbing in through the side window of her car. It was a big Plymouth, and I couldn't get the door open. I was on the passenger side, and she was in the driver's seat.'"

The woman still had a pulse, but she couldn't hold her head up. She was wheezing and struggling to breathe, so Jim leaned in and supported her neck in an attempt to stabilize the injury.

"She was slim and blonde, probably in her thirties, though it was so dark and there was so much blood that it was hard to tell. Her eyes met mine, and it was heartbreaking to see her. I knew the ambulance wouldn't make it in time, so I said, 'I'm not going to leave you. I'm right here by your side.' I told her we were going to try to get her out. I wanted to give her a glimmer of hope, even though the situation was hopeless. I just supported her head as she slowly slipped away. She died while I was holding her."

He tells me there was an atmosphere of sadness around that woman.

"For me, anyway. I guess it was probably just me projecting that onto her. But the whole thing was so tragic."

Her husband died on the way to the hospital, which meant that all three people involved in the crash ended up losing their lives.

"I experienced every emotion that night. I felt compassion for her and sadness that I didn't know whether she was Christian or not. I didn't know whether she had kids at home. I didn't know anything."

After the woman passed away, Jim started clearing the road because the traffic was blocked in both directions.

"That was when the anger hit me. No one else helped; they all just stood and stared. They pulled over, jumped out, and gawped. You know, at the blood and the rest of it, it was all pretty gory. The man in the smaller of the two cars had broken pretty much every bone in his body. It was terrible. But no one would help us. The funeral director and I were the only ones who did a thing, and that made me so mad. I said, 'I hope they get their fill.' I was irate. Sad for the people who had died and angry because we couldn't help them because we got there too late. I felt strongly that I didn't want her to die alone, and I was grateful she didn't have to— that I was there."

So, that was where it all began for you?

"That night, yes. If I hadn't been there, she would have died alone. But she didn't deserve that. No one deserves to die alone."

After the family moved to Bertram, Jim says that he and Janice agreed that he should pursue his master's degree at the seminary. He wanted to be able to give communion and do everything a pastor can for his congregation. He hungered for the word of God.

"That was my driving force, to get a master's degree in theology or pastoral theology. The problem was that the seminary was almost 150 miles from our home, and I drove there and back four days a week. That meant a lot of time behind the wheel. I drove nearly 300 miles a day to and from school, and then I kept studying once I got home. On top of that, I was also working full-time as a pastor."

Jim felt that he and Janice became more and more distant during this period.

"Have you ever heard the song 'When a Man Loves a Woman' by Percy Sledge?"

I nod.

"Well, that was how I felt. I'd pictured a life where I worked all day while my wife stayed at home. She would keep the house neat and tidy and have dinner and candles waiting for me when I got back. We'd eat a nice meal, relax, and enjoy each other's company."

That was how Jim thought married life should be, but reality proved different.

"We had no money at the time, and to make ends meet, she started childminding. Five days a week, she was stuck inside with a bunch of kids, which meant that when the weekend came around, she just wanted to get out of the house and do something fun together. She wanted to go roller-skating, anything. But I'd been rushing around all week, so I was dog-tired, and on Friday night, when she wanted to go out somewhere, we just ended up staying home."

What did that do to the marriage?

"It created a rift. I was demanding too much of her, things that I had been longing for all my life but that she couldn't give me. Looking back, I don't blame Janice at all. It was never her fault, but I didn't see that when I was younger. I failed her. I didn't realize it at the time, but I do now."

. . .

During his time at the seminary, Jim also found work as a hospital chaplain. One of his regular tasks there was to sit by people's bedsides as they died.

"Something that happened there really did change my life. It helped me get a better understanding of life and death. I was the chaplain at Baylor Hospital in Dallas, and I remember there was a middle-aged woman in the cancer ward. Everyone knew she was dying, that it was just a matter of time. I'd been to see her several times, and when I went in one day, they told me things weren't looking too good, so I sat by her bedside. Her family was there—her husband, son, and daughter—and it was clear that she was about to die. Her son had been there for four days straight and hadn't left the hospital once—not even the ward; he'd been by her side the whole time. People kept telling him, 'Son, you can't stay here forever. You need to eat and get some rest.' But he said, 'No, I don't want to.' Ultimately, they practically insisted he leave, and he gave in and headed home."

The family lived a thirty-minute drive from the hospital, and the woman died no more than two or three minutes after he left. This was back before everyone had cellphones, which meant his family couldn't reach him until he got home.

"When he found out she was dead, he slammed the phone down and raced back to the hospital. The rest of us talked as we waited for him. His sister and father were both crying, but they also laughed and told stories. I thought it was good that they were able to start grieving and process the fact that she was gone. I was standing by the door when it flew open, and the son came storming in. He grabbed me by the scruff of my neck and threw me across the bed. His father tried to get up, but the son pushed him back down and then walked over to his mother and straddled her and started hitting her."

Jim shakes his head.

"His own dead mother. I grabbed one arm, his father took the other, and we pulled him away from her and held him until he broke down in tears. Once he started crying, it was as though all his anger had melted away. He had been waiting for his mother to die for four days, but she had held out while he was there. He felt betrayed."

Jim tells me it was a long afternoon as they tried to calm him down.

"He hugged his dad and cried and cried and said he was sorry for pushing him. He also apologized to me. There was a beautiful moment after that when we all gathered around the bed. He gripped his mother's beautifully manicured hand, I held his other, and we said a prayer. We stood quietly, still hand in hand. You could really feel the love and the grief, the way it flowed through the room, and I knew the process had started. Ultimately, I saw the family out, and we left the mother in her room."

Around this time, Jim was also taking a class in Clinical Pastoral Education, in which participants were given an insight into everything that happens at a hospital. After saying goodbye to the grieving family that day, Jim met up with a few of his classmates to grab something to eat and talk through his experience. Midway through the meal, however, their pagers started beeping.

"We thought something serious must have happened, so we all jumped up. Our supervisor was waiting for us in the basement, and he said, 'Gentlemen, we're going to observe an autopsy.' I thought that sounded great."

They made their way into the autopsy room, where a covered body was waiting for them on the table.

"The pathologist started talking, then folded back one of the sheets to reveal the upper body. The person's face and lower body were still hidden at that point; all we could see was the torso."

It was a woman. The pathologist pressed the scalpel to her chest and began to make an incision.

"It was okay at first. I didn't feel much as I watched, even though I'd never seen the inside of a body before, but then he moved the sheet a little, and that's when I saw her hands. I immediately recognized her beautifully manicured nails because I'd been looking down at those same hands just an hour earlier."

Jim was looking at the hand he had held as the woman died.

"After that, it no longer felt clinical to me. It became too real. I nearly passed out on the spot and had to go out into the hallway. That woman gave me a real insight into life's beauty and how it's the small things that set the big thoughts whirring. It was no longer just a body; I'd known her, laughed with her, prayed with her, and watched her die. I had a lot to process that evening."

Why do you think that was so important to you?

"It can be a clinical experience to see a dead body, but if you knew that person, they become real again, and that means you have to be careful. It made me understand just how fragile we are. We might think we're resilient, but the vessel

God has given us is precious and delicate. I felt honored to have been a part of that in such an intimate way, and I felt a powerful connection to the family. I never saw them again after they left the hospital that day, but they've always been a part of me."

During his time at the hospital in Dallas, Jim also worked as a chaplain on the maternity ward.

"Oh, boy, that's another tough story. There were eighteen labor rooms and four delivery suites at that hospital, and one evening was so busy that there were heavily pregnant women on gurneys in the corridor. It was the night before Halloween, and I was enjoying going between the rooms. There was always something going on there. It's a heartening, exciting place to be, considering all the babies being born, and there was a couple who just seemed so happy. She was in pain, like all the other women, but they were also excited to welcome their baby. I went in and chatted with them for a while, then hurried off to talk with some of the others. The woman was taken through to the delivery suite and gave birth, but the doctor immediately realized something was wrong, and they called me back in. Everyone was so worried. The mother was still in bed, and I went through to the room where they were trying to save her baby. The doctors said, 'He's not going to make it,' and I stayed with them until the baby died."

Jim stood by and watched as they worked on the infant.

"My job in that instance is to do nothing. I just tried to stay out of the way. It was my job to provide support and do whatever they asked me to do once they eventually needed my help."

The hospital staff moved the parents into a quiet room, and Jim went to sit with them and said that the doctor was on his way.

"They wanted to know how their baby was doing, but I couldn't say anything. That was always so hard. In the end, the doctor came through and told them that he'd done everything he could but that he hadn't been able to save the boy. That was a full-term pregnancy with no obvious complications, and yet their baby was dead. Oh, they cried and cried."

The doctor asked whether they wanted to see their son, and the couple said yes. Jim went through to let the midwife know and found her in tears, so he sat down and chatted with her for a while.

"We prayed. I gave her my handkerchief, and we hugged; I told her the parents wanted to see their baby."

She got to work preparing the boy, but her hands were shaking so much that Jim took over and wrapped him in a blanket.

"I returned to the parents and put him in his mother's arms. She rocked him and said, 'How precious.' I wasn't sure whether I was allowed to leave them alone with him, but then the father got up and kissed the boy on the forehead. It was such a beautiful, heartbreaking, tender moment, witnessing their grief as they looked down at the baby with such love. I spent maybe ten minutes just standing there, and I knew they would be okay on their own for a while."

Jim decided to go and grab a coffee, and he talked a little more with the midwife. Whenever something like that happened, the mood in the maternity unit always changed. Everyone was upset, including the midwives, the doctors, and the rest of the staff.

"That really surprised me. I was stunned by how

affected they all were, but it was because they put their heart and soul into their work. I decided to stay there for the rest of my shift, just to be present for anyone who needed to talk, to do what I could to help."

He gave the couple an hour to themselves before he went back through to them.

"They had already started the grieving process. They'd made a few calls and told their relatives the news. Some of their family was on their way to the hospital, and the parents didn't want them to see the boy, so they asked me to take him away."

The hospital was short-staffed that evening, and the head nurse asked Jim if he could take the baby down to the morgue, where his body would be kept until autopsy.

"I said, 'Absolutely. How do I do that?' and the midwife grabbed a sheet. She was gentle with the boy, but she kind of crumpled it around him and told me to carry it as though I was heading to the laundry room."

Jim picked up the boy and went out into the corridor. He took the elevator down to the basement, made his way through to pathology, and handed the baby over to the doctor there.

"After that, I went back up to the parents and told them where he was. They were so grateful, broken, and full of despair, but they had their faith. They were strong enough to cope, and I knew they would learn to live with it. That felt good, despite everything."

Do all children go to Heaven?

. . .

"I think so. They haven't reached the age when they can take responsibility for their actions. That happens sometime around nine when you learn right from wrong. At that age, a child is receptive to the idea that God exists, and they're able to make an active decision as to whether He is part of their life or not. But until then, until they're capable of making that decision, all children go to Heaven."

What is it like to see a child die?

"You don't want to let them go. I've seen a lot of children die since that first baby. It's not as dramatic as it tends to be with adults. Their breathing doesn't rattle as much, and they don't fight it quite as much. There seems to be something peaceful about it; it's over far quicker. I've seen some real tragedies over the years. For example, we faced some heartbreaking situations at the church in Liberty Hill. In fact, during my time as a pastor at Bertram, I buried twenty-two children. That's tough."

He tells me that the saddest funeral he ever officiated was for one of his deacons' sons.

"He was a man I deeply respect, even now. He was so strong in his faith, and his love for his wife was wonderful. They had a very good life together."

Their first child was born with Down's Syndrome.

"Oh, they loved that little boy, and he loved everybody in the church. But when he was three, his heart gave out. They never really recovered from that. They just loved him so much."

The couple wanted to have another child, and though they tried and tried, nothing happened. In the end, they made the decision to adopt a boy from a troubled background instead.

"They welcomed that little boy into their lives and showed him so much love, but he really didn't have an easy time of it. I think he was four when he came to them, and they loved him as though he was their own, but he struggled to build a connection with them. Just as he finally began to warm to them, she discovered she was pregnant, and they had another son, Timothy. Their love for that baby was boundless."

Every spring, the area where the family lived held a Little League tournament.

"Little League was a big deal in Liberty Hill, and both their boys played. Timothy had a game early that morning, so they split into two vehicles. The adopted boy and the mom were in one car, and Timothy and the dad were in the pickup. They drove to their respective games, and once play was over, they headed home again. Timothy said, 'Daddy, can I ride in the back?'

"In those days, everyone in the country thought it was okay to drive around with their kids in the back of the truck. The house was just a little over a mile away, and everything went smoothly. The only problem was that one of the neighbors had a big tree right by the driveway to their house, which meant they couldn't see if there was any traffic coming when they reversed out. There almost never was, but on that particular day, they pulled out right in front of the pickup as it approached.

"The father skidded and hit the ditch, and the pickup tipped as he tried to swing back up onto the road. Timothy was thrown out of the back, and the truck rolled right on top of him. The ambulance arrived in no time at all, and they loaded him into the back and sped away. They called me, and I headed straight to the hospital. He was still alive when I ran into the room where they were fighting to save his life, and I reached out and grabbed his hand. He was this sweet little boy who never missed a single Sunday School session. He was always in church. Such a funny little guy. He died as I held his hand."

Jim asked the doctor if he could be the one to tell the parents, and the doctor said he would be grateful if he did.

"So, I went through to the room where they were waiting. They stood up as I came in, and we all sat down together. I told them that Timothy had just passed. They broke down in tears, as you can imagine, and the father was overcome by guilt. It was just such a terrible, terrible accident."

Guilt must be one of the emotions you come into contact with most.

"Guilt is a big part of my life. People want to talk about it all the time. For those who are doing time, the guilt they carry is often a worse prison than the physical walls surrounding them."

. . .

What do you say to a parent who was inadvertently responsible for their child's death?

"It's more a question of what I don't say. I'd never say 'I know how you feel,' for example, because I don't."

Jim pauses and considers his words.

"I don't try to identify with them. I hug them and tell them that I'm so sorry about what they're going through, and then I try to get them to look at the bigger picture and reach a place where they understand that it wasn't intentional. That can take some time, though."

How does a person move on from that kind of guilt? How do they learn to live with it?

"When it comes to the grieving process, guilt is often the most difficult thing to grapple with. Thoughts like, 'If only I'd done this or that.' Guilt clogs a person's heart and mind, and it can lead to anger toward other people. When we're racked with feelings of guilt, we often say cruel things to one another—things we don't actually mean—just to ease the pain temporarily. At the heart of guilt, there's a belief that you've done something unforgivable—like Timothy's father letting him sit in the bed of the pickup—and you have to try to reach a point where you understand that it's actually something you can forgive yourself for. That the decision you made can be forgiven. It's about finding the key to your own guilt and unlocking the chains holding you down."

. . .

But how does someone actually go about that?

"In my experience, it's about returning to the moment and facing the guilt head-on—really looking at your actions, whatever you did, until you spot the key. That's where you'll find it, where you'll find forgiveness. If a person can face down all the emotions that stir up and then take concrete steps to process and work through them, they'll find forgiveness."

The parents wanted to see their son, so Jim went through to the room where Timothy was laid out. He found one of the nurses in tears on the floor, and he sat down beside her and put an arm around her shoulders. They sat there together for some time, and the nurse told him she had done her best for Timothy, that he was such a precious child.

"She just kept repeating the same thing over and over, and I let her talk for a while before telling her that the parents wanted to see him."

Jim went over to the boy, cleaned his face, and made him look as presentable as possible. He then turned out most of the lights in an attempt to hide the worst of his injuries, pulled a sheet over him, and closed his eyes.

"After that, I went back through to his parents. We went in together, and they were admirably composed. The father stood on one side of the boy, and the mother on the other."

Their surviving son wasn't with them—they hadn't wanted him to come—so the three of them were alone in the room. They held hands and prayed.

"I remember the father looked up at me and said, 'You'll

conduct the funeral, won't you?' I said that, of course, I would, that I'd do whatever they asked. We talked a little about the ceremony, and they both cried and prayed. I decided to leave the room at that point to give them a moment with him."

The funeral home was in Georgetown, around fifteen miles away, but the funeral itself would be held in Liberty Hill.

"We thought it was crazy to have a viewing in George-town, making everyone drive all the way there and back again to see the body before holding the ceremony in Liberty Hill the next day. The funeral director agreed to let us have an open casket in the church instead, on the condition that someone stayed with the boy at all times—including overnight. I couldn't ask the parents to do that; I just couldn't, so I said I would stay."

They placed the open casket in the large foyer of the church, and the mourners filed in to see him and then went through to the congregation hall to pray with the family.

"I think everyone who lived in Liberty Hill came out to see Timothy that evening."

In Sweden, having an open casket at a funeral is very unusual. Why do you think people here want to see a dead body?

"To say goodbye. It needs to sink in. Personally, I've always thought that's harder if you haven't seen the body."

· · ·

Back home, it's the other way around. Almost no one has an open casket, and on the few occasions it does happen, everyone has to be informed and prepared in advance because it could be traumatic. That applies to the priest and the janitor, the church musicians, and the mourners. Everyone has to know the casket will be open before they arrive."

"Almost all funerals here involve an open casket. If I can't see that someone is dead, I might get it into my head that they're not really gone and that I'll see them again someday. It's not so bad now, but when I was younger, it was. I had a real problem with it for a long time, and I know of plenty of people who have suffered because they couldn't say a proper goodbye. One mother almost lost her mind because she never saw her daughter in the coffin. She refused to believe she was really dead. I think it brings people closure to be able to see a dead body."

That evening, after the viewing, Jim locked the church doors and lay down to sleep in the same room as Timothy.

"It wasn't easy being there with him; it was as though I kept expecting to hear him move or breathe, even though I knew he wouldn't. I actually talked to him during the night. I told him he was a lucky young man for having parents who loved him so much and for giving him such a rich, happy life. And early the next morning, I got up to prepare for the funeral."

People started to arrive two hours before the ceremony was due to begin. The church could seat 350, and once the pews were full, it was standing room only. In the end, between 500 and 600 mourners attended that day.

"It seems that everything that could go wrong did go wrong. A few years later their older son really struggled with his grief and so his life spiraled into a very hard adulthood. Then Dick, one of the finest men I have ever known, died suddenly. His loving and strong wife had to carry on. She has done a wonderful job holding the family together. I couldn't imagine what it would be like to go through what she did."

What would you say you've learned from all these people you've seen die in hospitals, car wrecks, and execution chambers?

"They taught me that death is nothing to be afraid of. I'm not at all scared to die. They taught me that there are far worse things than death."

Like what?

"Like being stuck in prison for the rest of your life. That's worse than death—or never seeing your family again, never being able to hug them. That's worse than death. I'm grateful for the life I have, and I've seen people die without knowing God. I've met people who are angry with God and who have turned their back on Him before they died. I've met people who spent their entire lives loving Him with all their heart and passed away with unwavering faith."

As a Swede, it's fascinating to hear how big a role God plays in the United States. According to the latest statistics, only twenty-four percent of the Swedish population identify as Christian, but in the U.S., the figure is sixty-four percent. In Sweden, not even the Christian Democrats talk about God, but here, it's unthinkable for a politician not to be a believer. People would never vote for them.

"What can I say? God makes a difference. When death comes knocking, God makes a difference. That's what I've learned from seeing hundreds of people die."

It took Jim five long years to get his master's degree, and when he left the seminary in 1980, he felt like he had reached the top.

"God taught me several very important lessons during that time. When I graduated, I felt like I'd finally achieved what I wanted to achieve in life. I finished in May, and Janice was pregnant with our youngest daughter. We'd had our second child, Brian, in 1976. When Misty was born, our first, I wasn't allowed to be present for the birth, but that had changed by the time he came along, and I was with her for the whole thing. I held her hand as he saw the light of day for the first time. And then it was Jana's turn. By then, I'd finished my EMT training and was already working as a first responder at car accidents and that sort of thing. Because of that, I started joking with the doctor. I said, 'Well, you know, I learned how to deliver a baby, so I thought—considering how much it costs to give birth in this country—I'd save some money and deliver the little one myself.' We laughed, and then he went on his way."

Not long later, however, a nurse came over to Jim.

"Mr. Brazzil? The doctor would like to see you in his office."

Jim was terrified and immediately thought something must be wrong. He hurried through the hospital and knocked on the door, letting himself in as soon as he heard the doctor's voice. On the other side, he found the doctor standing in his underpants. An embarrassed Jim apologized, but the doctor just waved him in and said, "We need to get ready."

"He threw me a set of clothes. I pulled them on, and then he asked me if I knew how to scrub in. I said that I'd seen people do it a few times, and he told me to follow his lead and that he would show me what to do. We both scrubbed in, and once we were done, the rest of the team was waiting with our operating room gowns. They got me into mine, and he asked, 'Are you right or left-handed?' That was when I realized something unusual was happening."

Jim told the doctor he was right-handed, and the doctor called to the delivery suite, "Put the tray on the right-hand side."

The two men then made their way through to Janice, who was already lying with her legs in the stirrups. The doctor moved over to the corner and said, "Just let me know if you need anything."

Jim smiles at the memory.

"I got to deliver Jana. It was a straightforward birth, and

everything went smoothly. I lifted her onto Janice's chest as soon as she came out."

The doctor worked with Jim to examine the girl, and Jim then cut the umbilical cord.

"After that, he said, 'Once she delivers the placenta, we'll get the episiotomy fixed up.' Janice hadn't uttered a word so far, but at that, she opened her mouth and said, 'I think it'd be better if you did that,' to the doctor."

Jim laughs so hard that he has to dry his eyes.

"I didn't get to suture Janice, but I did do everything else, and my goodness, that birth was such a wonderful experience. Jana and I have had a special bond ever since."

Chapter Seven

I'd failed God and couldn't tell anyone about it.

1981-1984

Three weeks after Jana was born, after seven years of long drives, three jobs, studying at the seminary, and marital tension, the Brazzil family moved to the more prosperous San Antonio suburb of Bulverde.

"Life took a real turn in Bulverde. I moved there for the prestige, I guess. I thought it would be great. I had my master's degree, and I had my family; I had three children and a beautiful wife, and I thought I'd made it. I thought, 'Life is good.' I turned away from God, and that was the biggest mistake I could have made. It's probably the biggest mistake I ever made."

Jim threw himself into his work at the church, doing his best to be a good pastor.

"Bulverde was a very different type of place. There were five millionaires in the congregation. These people were first class through and through."

For Jim, who had always struggled with his poor upbringing and his inferiority complex, that came as a real culture shock.

"The congregation members weren't warm and friendly; they were more businesslike. They weren't keen on pitching in to help and would rather pay someone else to do the job. That didn't really sit well with me, so I never truly felt like I fit in there."

Despite all that, it was in Bulverde that he came into contact with the State Corrections System for the first time.

"A guy in my congregation said he was interested in visiting prisons, so I contacted the Sheriff's Department in San Antonio. With his blessing, we started going to the county jails once a week."

Jim tells me he felt incredibly nervous ahead of his first trip.

"Prison wasn't something I knew much about. No one I knew had been to prison, and I'd never even visited one. I had no idea what to expect."

As it happened, he loved it from the moment he set foot inside.

"It was amazing. The place was full of angry young men, up to eight in every cell, but being able to sit down with a few of them and pray together really opened my eyes."

What did you like about it?

"Nothing was fake there. Everyone was wearing the same clothes. I was used to spending time around my well-dressed congregation, so I immediately felt more comfortable surrounded by prison uniforms than all those crisp shirts. The men's emotions were all pretty raw, too, because they hadn't been there so long. Their crimes were still fresh, and they were young and malleable. Going in there as a pastor, they knew what I wanted. They listened to me and treated me with respect. We talked about real things. I never asked why they were there, but they always told me anyway. I didn't judge them; I just tried to give them a sense of hope and faith and something to live for. Those men taught me so much. They made me realize that a person's relationship with God has nothing to do with the church. The church is simply a tool God uses to help us grow and become stronger. Prison isn't a place of prestige or affluence; it's a place where people need love and grace."

After moving to Bulverde, Janice stayed home with their newborn daughter, and their marital problems continued.

"A woman came to see me at my office one day. I offered counseling, and she and her husband were going through a rough patch. During those sessions with people, I never sat behind my desk. I didn't want them to see me as a figure of authority, so I used to sit in an armchair. This woman was really beautiful, and after our chat, she said, 'Brother Jim, you've been so good to me. Is there anything I can do for you in return?'"

Jim immediately understood the type of favor she was offering him. And he accepted.

"I was weak. There is no other way around it."

Jim tells me he felt overwhelmed afterward, that a feeling of distress washed over him.

"I knew how grubby it was. I felt trapped—like I had nowhere to go. I'd failed God and couldn't tell anyone about it. She was beautiful, and it had been nice, but it also felt like I had manipulated her into doing it."

A week later, the same woman called and said they needed to talk. She came to Jim's office, and he felt incredibly embarrassed and didn't know what to do with himself. The woman said that she wanted to continue the affair with him. Jim was stunned and told her it wasn't a good idea, that he was married—and so was she. He reminded her that she had two beautiful children and that this was the last thing either of them needed.

"She said that if I didn't do it, she would tell her husband what happened. And so we ended up having an affair. It was awful."

Forgive the cynicism, but that sounds like a bit of an excuse to me. It's all a little "poor me for having to cheat on my wife."

"I know it does, but I didn't want to do it. I knew I had betrayed my wife and betrayed God. I'd betrayed myself and gotten into a situation where I was being blackmailed."

According to Jim, things rapidly got worse.

"She came to my office and said she wanted to get married, that she'd give me a million dollars if I left my wife

100

and kids and ran away with her. I told her that wasn't going to happen, and she threatened to tell her husband again. I asked her for some time to think, and then I went home, prayed to God, and agonized over what to do."

Two days later, Jim got a call from one of his deacons. The man said he wanted to go for a drive so they could talk, and once they were in the car together, he explained that the woman had been in touch and told him everything.

"In the vast majority of churches, I would have been fired right there and then, but I told them I would leave voluntarily if they agreed not to do that. And they did."

I'm having a little trouble feeling any sympathy for you here.

"That's okay. I don't need any sympathy. I made a horrible mistake."

Jim told Janice what had happened.

There was plenty of anger and tears, but there was also forgiveness.

"I think we should move back home," she said.

And so that was what they did.

Jim Brazzil resigned from his post in Bulverde, and the family returned to Bertram.

Chapter Eight

I let go of my anger, and I moved on.
I found my feet in my current circumstances and felt at ease.

1984-1995

Back in Bertram, Jim had plans to take another clinical pastoral training course while also working as a chaplain at a hospital. On his first day on the job, however, he was handed a letter announcing that all non-revenue generating activities at the hospital—including the chaplaincy service—would be cut due to a lack of funds. Yet again, he found himself in a new home with a family to support and bills to pay but no job or money.

He got in touch with another hospital, St. David's, and found a position in the maintenance department. After three and a half years at college, five years as a pastor, and a post-graduate degree in Bible Studies, he was right back where he started: working as a janitor at a hospital.

"I fixed problems with the ventilation, the drains, and that kind of thing. It was terrible, a real low-paying job. I'd been to every hospital in Texas, to the emergency rooms and operating theaters; I'd visited all sorts of wards in my role as a chaplain, and I thought I'd done it well, yet here I was working as a janitor again. It felt like I'd let God down—like I'd blown everything."

Jim tells me that he didn't place any blame on the woman from the church. Instead, he was angry with himself, and he was angry with his wife.

"I was angry because she wasn't acting the way I thought a married woman should. Intimacy, for instance. It felt like she was dangling it in front of me and giving me no more than a taste now and then. That's how I felt. I was angry with her."

That sounds pretty awful, "dangling it in front of me." As though men are animals who just can't help themselves, and the woman simply has to step up.

"That's what I thought at the time. I don't think that now."

It took him a while to overcome his anger and understand his part in everything.

"Once I realized it wasn't her fault, that I'd betrayed her and drifted away from God and let him down too... that's when I understood how many people I'd hurt with my affair and that it was okay to work as a janitor. I felt as though I was doing penance for my behavior."

Is your God a vengeful god?

"It wasn't so much punishment as penance. I realized that the person who had gotten me into that situation was me."

Jim sent his resumé to several churches in the hopes that one might employ him, but he had no real expectation of ever being able to work as a pastor again.

During an early morning shift one day, he got a call from the third floor to report a blocked toilet. Jim Brazzil grabbed his plunger, put it in a garbage bag so no one knew what it was, and headed up there. One of the nurses pointed to a hallway where two men were standing. He asked why they were there, and she said he would find out soon enough.

"I walked over to them, and it turned out the wife of the Governor of Texas had just had surgery. The two men were security guards who wanted to search me before I went in. I think I probably felt more humiliated in that moment than I ever have before. Here I was, a pastor with a master's degree, and they wanted to frisk me so that I could go in and unclog a toilet."

When he finally got inside, Jim was met by the worst stench he had ever encountered. Turning on the bathroom light, he saw that the toilet had overflowed, and feces and toilet paper were all over the floor. He had to wade through the water as he made his way across the room.

"That was the lowest point of my entire life, no doubt about it. I got to work, but I quickly broke down. I dropped to my knees in the awful mess and burst into tears. I said, 'God, I know I've sinned; I know I've disappointed you, and I understand that I've ruined everything. I made it so far along the road to becoming the pastor I was born to be, and now I'm sitting here in this foul mess.' That was exactly how I felt. And that was literally what I was doing: kneeling in poop. I told him, 'I don't know what else I can do but give up.'"

That was when he heard God's voice.

"I'm not saying I literally heard His voice, that He was talking aloud, but I heard Him all the same, and He said, 'Jim, I don't care whether you're preaching in the world's biggest church or scrubbing toilets at St. David's. If you do what I want you to do, everything will be just fine.'"

Jim says it was as though a soft breeze blew all around him, and he felt a sense of peace, unlike anything he had ever experienced before.

"I leaned against the plunger and said, 'Thank you, God, for hearing my prayers.' Then I got up and cleaned that bathroom—I left it sparkling. I picked up all the used toilet paper, all the mess, everything. I flushed it all, and then I rinsed off in the tub, double-checked I was presentable, closed the door behind me, and crept out."

When he left the hospital that day, Jim felt at peace, as though he could spend the rest of his life unblocking toilets.

"I let go of my anger, and I moved on. I found my feet in my current circumstances and felt at ease."

But before long, however, another door opened.

The very next week, Jim got a phone call. The First Baptist Church in Liberty Hill was looking for a pastor, and they asked whether he would be interested in taking the job. Jim went there to give a sermon, and the congregation liked what they heard. Just one month after he knelt by the overflowing toilet, he was named the new pastor at a church less than fifteen miles from his home in Bertram.

He describes his first sermon there as like finding a second wind; it felt refreshing.

"I chose a passage from Ezekiel. In it, he is gazing out across a valley; all he can see are sun-bleached bones. God says to him, 'Son of man, can these bones live?' I don't think that was a message to the churchgoers but to me: the idea that, in God's hands, nothingness and death can become life. That was what I felt. I was utterly lifeless and empty, and God gave me a second chance."

Jim felt a deep sense of gratitude.

"Some of the young men I met when I first started visiting prisons in Bulverde had done stupid things when they were eighteen or nineteen, and they ended up being stuck in the system for years as a result of that one mistake. But I'd done something stupid, too, and I'd been given another chance. I left Bulverde like a fish out of water. My calling was to make a difference in people's lives, and when I arrived in Liberty Hill, I found people with the same needs as me: to be forgiven and get a second chance. I felt like God had given me those experiences to prepare me."

Does everyone deserve a second chance?

"Yes."

· · ·

Without exception?

"When it comes to God, yes. Between people, things are different. If somebody hurt one of my children, for example, I'm not sure I would have been capable of giving them a second chance. But God does things we can't."

Jim loved the church in Liberty Hill so much that he ended up spending almost ten years as the pastor there, from 1985 to 1994. But on the home front, things were nowhere near as happy.

"Our marriage... Things weren't good before then, but they just got worse and worse. And I know that these days, as a pastor, I talk and talk and love to hear my own voice, but in my marriage back then there was little talking. I don't think I asked her the right questions and she didn't tell me how she felt. Things were just tough for us. And any closeness we might have had was gone."

One day, as Jim was reading *The Baptist Standard*, a Christian paper, he came across an article about a trip a group of pastors had made to Russia and Ukraine to visit prisoners there.

"I knew that Russia had been shut off from the world for years during the Soviet era and that it wasn't easy to get ahold of a Bible there. Reading that article, I thought, 'Wow, what an experience that would be, to go over there and give them the same hope God has given me."

Jim Brazzil showed the article to his secretary and said

that a trip of that kind would be a real blessing. She didn't seem to share his opinion that a few weeks' travel around the Russian prison system was a gift from God, and the conversation quickly fizzled out. Jim put the paper to one side and didn't give it any more thought until a week later, during a meeting at the church.

"There must have been at least sixty people there that evening. We were midway through the meeting, and as usual, I was the moderator. We'd reached the end of the agenda when one of my deacons stood up and said, 'Brother Jim, we'd like you to step out for a moment.' I thought they were about to fire me."

He did as he was told, feverishly trying to work out what he could have done wrong. The number of visitors to the church had dropped lately, and Jim felt as though he had failed God. He went to his office and sat down to wait to be told that his services were no longer needed.

"A few minutes later, someone came in and said, 'They're ready for you now.' I headed back through, fully expecting the worst. But to my surprise, a man said, 'Brother Jim, we hear you'd like to visit Russia and Ukraine, that you want to do missionary work there?' I said I did, and he continued, 'The church has voted unanimously to help get you there. We won't take it out of the church budget, but we're planning to organize several fundraisers to finance your trip.' I was so touched. They held garage sales, bake sales, all kinds of things, and in the end, they made enough money for me to go."

The trip took place in November 1992 and lasted two and a half weeks. Many of the communist regimes had only recently fallen, and there was a special atmosphere as West and East attempted to reconcile.

"If only you knew what I experienced there. I think we visited thirteen different prisons, and at each, we were taken to the warden's office first. There was always the exact number of chairs ready and waiting for us. They knew precisely who was coming because the KGB followed us everywhere. Those prisons were nothing like ours. The inmates barely got any food, nothing but bread and soup. If they managed to get their hands on anything else, it was something their relatives had brought them, but the vast majority never got any visits at all. Their eyes were so cold, so empty."

During the first visit of the trip, Jim gave a sermon—through an interpreter—from Acts, chapter 16, about Paul and Silas spending time in prison. They had been beaten for preaching and locked in a cell, and at midnight, the two men sang songs of praise to God as thanks for allowing them to share the word of Jesus. Suddenly, there was a powerful earthquake, and everyone was freed from their shackles. The prison guard, afraid he was going to be killed by the inmates, asked Paul and Silas what he should do, and they told him that Jesus would save him and offer him eternal life.

"When you go to a prison, you meet some of the most brutal individuals—murderers and other serious criminals. Their hearts are empty, but I told them that if they believed in Jesus, He would forgive them and help them find a new life. That was essentially the sermon I gave."

The room was packed that day, with 225 prisoners in attendance.

Jim said: "If you are willing to give your heart to Jesus, I don't care whether you're rich or poor, young or old, or someone who has never taken the Lord Jesus Christ as your savior; you need Him. Is anyone willing to stand up and tell everyone else in this room that they give their heart to Jesus?"

The warden was the first to get to his feet, and in the minutes that followed, 181 more men stood up—all prisoners.

"It was an incredible sight, watching them get up like that, one by one, to give themselves to Jesus."

And you don't think they did it because they were copying the warden?

"They were sincere, and the reason I know that is there were so many tears and emotions on show. And in prison, crying is something you just don't do."

Jim started handing out Bibles to the men who had stood up. Everyone wanted his autograph.

"I noticed that the crowd had begun to part slightly, and I looked up and saw the warden standing right in front of me. He wanted me to sign his Bible, so I opened it and wrote my name, and after handing it back, he reached out, grabbed my shoulders, and kissed me on the lips. I was kind of taken aback, and after that was all over, one of my fellow travelers leaned over to me and whispered that bad breath is the same in all languages."

Do you remember what was on your mind as you stood in front of all those prisoners?

. . .

"I was incredibly humbled by the idea that God could use my voice to touch so many people. The reaction was the same wherever we went on that trip. We headed over there with 4,500 Russian Bibles and didn't take a single one home."

That trip was what finally made Jim understand what God wanted from him: that he was meant to work with prisoners.

The command came straight from the Lord.

"It was the same voice I heard at the hospital that time while I was mopping up poop. God said, 'You're going to start working in prisons, and you are going to have many opportunities to be involved with and experience me.' I knew with absolute certainty that it was God calling to me, that it was Him talking. There was such an overwhelming sense of peace and a knowledge of what was going to happen. I said: 'Okay, you've spoken to me before, and you told me to trust you, which I did. You haven't let me down yet. I'll trust you again."

On the plane back to Texas, Jim was utterly at peace. He had a new direction and purpose in life, and it felt like he was finally about to turn a new page.

"I landed in Dallas on a Friday. My mom and uncle came to pick me up from the airport, but Janice wasn't there. That was when I knew something was really wrong. I was hurt because there was so much I wanted to tell her. My heart was full of gratitude and so much else, but she didn't even come to Dallas until the next day. I wanted us to be alone, but she said, 'I can't. I don't love you anymore.' Oh, boy. I'd been full to the brim a second earlier, but I felt utterly empty after that. She said, 'I dread going to bed with you. I dread getting up and seeing you in the morning. I don't want you to touch me, and I don't want to touch you.'"

He trails off.

"I took her for granted. I regret that."

Jim begged her to give their marriage another chance. Janice agreed to stay—at least for the time being.

"I thought that everything would be different if we could just get away from Liberty Hill."

He started looking for jobs in correctional facilities and quickly discovered just how much lower the wages were inside the prison walls.

"If I wanted to work as a prison chaplain, I would have to take a fifty percent pay cut, which I couldn't really afford. On the other hand, God had told me to do it. I was following His will, but I also went through a bit of a crisis of faith. I honestly didn't know how I would be able to support my family."

Jim applied for jobs with several prisons, but each one turned him down. In the end, two years after his trip to Russia and Ukraine, he got a call about a job as a chaplain at the Wynne Unit in Huntsville. It was three hours east of Liberty Hill.

"I was still living with Janice at the time, and I hoped that everything would get better once we moved to Huntsville. Looking back, that was a very unrealistic thought, but I had very firm beliefs when it comes to the nuclear family and I was not ready to give up on those."

It was December 1994 when Jim Brazzil got the job in Huntsville, but Janice said she wanted to stay in Liberty Hill until the next summer to see out the academic year at the school where she worked. Jim suspected that wasn't the real reason, but there was little he could do to change her mind. He moved into a trailer in Huntsville and began his very first job as a prison chaplain.

"I can still picture that first day like a scene from a movie. God had spoken to me beforehand and told me this was what I was meant to be doing, but I just felt so unsure. I remember walking down a hallway toward the chapel, and the inmates who worked in the laundry were lined up against the wall. They laughed as I passed, and that scared me. It didn't feel anything like my visit to the prison in Bulverde. These were hardened criminals who would spend many years—possibly even the rest of their lives—behind bars. They had nothing left to lose, and that felt so big and frightening. I thought, 'I'm not in the right place here. What am I doing?'"

Not long after, he got a call from the chaplain at another Huntsville prison, the Ellis Unit. The chaplain asked whether Jim would be willing to come and hold a class there.

"This was before I ever even considered working on death row, which was based out of Ellis at the time. I was afraid, but I said I would do it."

He still remembers walking down the long main corridor, with entrances to various wings along both sides. The place was like a labyrinth, but he soon found himself standing outside of death row for the first time.

Jim hesitated for a few seconds, looking up at the blue bars that separated the condemned inmates from the rest of the prisoners. Then he went into the office to ask for help finding where his course was due to take place.

"You going to the chapel?' someone asked.

Jim nodded, and the guard unlocked the door. They rounded the corner and came to yet another door. As before, the guard opened it for him, and Jim stepped into another room, around sixteen feet wide and thirty feet long.

"Once I was inside, the guard brought in the inmates."

There were twenty death row prisoners present that day, and Jim found himself wondering what on earth he was doing there.

"I had assumed there would be as many guards as there were inmates, but there was only one. He looked at me and said I had two hours; then he went on his way. I heard him lock the door behind me."

As he stood there, Jim realized that every single one of the men in front of him had killed someone and that they were all going to die sometime soon.

"I wondered what I could possibly have to offer them, these tough criminals who'd been sentenced to death for murder. I felt so empty. And then I opened my mouth and told them the truth. I said, 'I'm terrified to be here. You're all violent criminals. You could kill me in the blink of an eye if you wanted to, but I'm here to bring you the good news about Jesus Christ and to let you know that God sees you. He has a use for you here."

Jim told the men about the prisoners he visited in Russia and Ukraine and about the impression that trip had made on him. He also introduced them to a book—*Experiencing God*—that he had come across there.

"They were really interested in that and said they

wanted to learn more. I ended up giving three talks about that book there. It was fantastic just to visit with those men and see and feel... I can still remember the suffocating smell of the place. The Ellis Unit is an old prison, and it smells so musty and stifling. I loved it."

Jim's father died in February 1995, so he took some time off work to officiate the funeral.

"It was a difficult time for me. I lost my dad, and my wife was still refusing to move to Huntsville, which meant I couldn't see the kids every day. And though I loved my new job at the prison, I also missed being a pastor in the church. It all just felt like a tremendous loss—a hodgepodge of loneliness and helplessness."

Summer came and went, and Janice continued to make excuses as to why she couldn't move. Jim realized she would probably never come to Huntsville, but he wasn't prepared to give up.

"I went and talked to my boss. The correctional system was growing at the time, which meant there were always new prisons popping up all over the place, and he told me that there were plans to open a women's prison in Gatesville."

Gatesville was only an hour and fifteen minutes from Liberty Hill and just a few miles from Jim's mother. Jim thought that Janice might agree to move there. It was close enough to be able to keep in touch with old friends, but it would also mean a new start for their marriage.

The prospect of being closer to his family convinced Jim to apply for the job at Woodman State Jail in Gatesville, and he was successful. The prison was still being built, but Jim drove over there to find an apartment, hoping his wife would join him.

"I called Janice that Thursday evening just to talk. She told me that my boss had been trying to get in touch with me. I didn't have a cellphone at the time, and it was already after five in the evening, so I wasn't sure how to call him back."

As luck would have it, Janice had given the boss the number for Jim's new apartment in Gatesville, and he called again at six thirty the next morning. The boss said he needed Jim in the office at 8:30 the next day.

"It was a Friday, and I was three hours away, so I told him I couldn't make it, that I had a trailer full of furniture, a few vacation days to take, and that I needed to unpack my things. He asked how soon I could be there, and I said Monday. I also asked him why, given I was meant to be on leave."

The boss didn't want to get into it over the phone, he just told Jim to come in on Monday morning, to bring two suits, and to be prepared to stay for several days.

Over the weekend, Jim hauled everything into his new apartment in Gatesville. On Monday morning, he got up at four to drive back to Huntsville, where the Director of Chaplains surprised him with the responsibility of working his very first execution and the offer of a job as the chaplain on death row. All of which takes us back to the garage in Huntsville, where Jim spent three days praying to God.

So, after those three days, you went to the warden and accepted the job. What happened next?

. . .

"I went through to my office and felt pretty validated. I think I already mentioned the empty drawers there, that the previous chaplain took everything when he left. Well, that meant I had to start from scratch. In some ways, I'm grateful for that because it meant I didn't have to follow in his footsteps. I could forge my own path instead. I thought a lot about the purpose and direction I wanted to take."

His conversation with God and the experience of meeting so many prisoners in Russia and Ukraine had left a real impression on him. Jim's job was to change people's lives, not just temporarily. Spending time with the death row inmates during their last few hours was a key part of that, but there were also plenty of other prisoners who weren't scheduled to die on any given day, and he wanted to give them a chance to change in their hearts and souls.

"I wanted it to be a real turning point in their lives, a genuine discipleship. That was my aim as their chaplain."

Ambitious. And beautiful.

"There's an old saying that goes, 'If you always do what you've always done, you'll always get what you've already got.' It might not be good grammar, but it's the thought that counts. I wanted to be able to break the cycle, and it was also a new start for me."

The new job brought him freedom.

"Being a chaplain within the correctional system is completely different from being the pastor of a regular congregation. As the pastor of a church, you're independent because the Baptist church is independent. The local church

117

pays your wage, and it decides whether or not you get to stay. That means if the old ladies aren't happy with you, you won't be able to keep the job for long. You don't dare push too hard in your sermons because you don't want to upset anyone, but in prison, I quickly learned that the inmates had no say over whether or not I got paid every month."

So you could go further?

"Exactly. I had the freedom to tell them a few home truths, and I did. I actually called them out from time to time. Many of the men who came to the chapel brought smuggled items with them, and they bartered with the others there. They hid cans and cigarettes in their socks and underwear, and that wasn't all. A few of them got up to homosexual acts, too. I caught them at it one day, two prisoners with their hands in each other's pants. I said, 'I don't care whether you're gay, Christian or not; the chapel is God's house. You can't come here to play your homosexual games. You can't come here to play with your boyfriends or girlfriends. This is God's house. And if you can't come here and respect His presence, you aren't welcome here.' All the other inmates stood up and clapped, and the two men straightened their clothes, got up, and left."

What do you mean by "homosexual games?"

. . .

"There are a lot of older men in prison who aren't actually gay; they just do it for the money. It's a game to them. Some really are homosexual, of course. I knew a guy on the Wynne Unit who was. He told me that he'd had the chance to get out but decided it was safer to be in prison than out in the free world. He got three meals a day there, clothes, health insurance, and he also earned pretty well from selling sex. He was happy."

Jim says that for the first time in a long while, he got to do real pastoral work.

"It was deeply satisfying to spend time with those people on death row. Not because they were going to die, but because... you know, how often do you get a chance to sit down and really talk to someone? I gained their trust over the months and years leading up to their executions, and then, when the time came, I could look them in the eye and say, 'In a few hours, you're going to die. You need to put your affairs in order with Jesus; otherwise, you won't get to Heaven. There's no time to play games. Either you're guilty, or you're not. You don't have to tell me, but you need to reconcile with God. Now is the time for you to open your heart to Him; if you do that, you can make a real difference.' To me, that was real pastoral work. It got right to the nitty gritty."

Jim's work continued to go well, but the same couldn't be said of his home life. Janice was still refusing to move to Huntsville.

"The winter of 1995 was a tough time for me. My daughter Misty was pregnant with her second child, and I lived so far away. That Christmas was a real mess. I celebrated with my mom, but it was just the two of us; my family

119

wasn't there. I felt so down."

His three children came to visit him in Huntsville not long after the holidays.

"That was probably what saved me. We spent some quality time together. We talked and cried over the fact that my marriage was falling apart and that our family would never be the same again. I often think of 1995 as the year of loss because that's when I lost so many things, but I also gained the job that would be the most meaningful thing in my life."

Chapter Nine

The moment he died, I felt an overwhelming sense of relief.

I'm not ashamed to admit that.
It was a good thing he had finally left this earth.

1995-1996

In the beginning, at the first few executions he attended, Jim Brazzil wanted to know everything in advance. He read up on all the grizzly details of the condemned inmates' crimes in an attempt to really understand them.

But at his eighth execution, he found himself face to face with an inmate by the name of Kenneth Granviel, a man who had broken into a woman's home and murdered her and her two-year-old daughter. Shortly after their deaths, a couple of the woman's friends—accompanied by a three-year-old boy—rang the bell. Granviel let them in and then proceeded to kill all three with a carving knife. He later went on to confess to the murders of another two women and led law enforcement officers to their bodies.

"I went into that room and felt such a powerful dislike for him. I tried to talk to him about God's love, forgiveness, and reconciliation... but it all just fell flat. The more I tried, the hollower my words sounded. Ultimately, I couldn't bear to spend another minute with him. I came up with an excuse and walked away... just left. And once I was outside, I dropped to my knees behind a fence and spent the next forty-five minutes throwing up, crying, and praying."

Jim went to talk to the prison warden, who bluntly told him to get back inside and do his job.

"So, I went through to the death house and sat down and talked with the prisoner again. I told him I was having a hard time dealing with his crimes and apologized for that, then said that my role was to focus on his needs rather than his crimes."

As Jim heard those words leave his mouth, his perspective shifted. He realized that the condemned inmate was looking at Jim Brazzil, the man, when he should have been dealing with Pastor Jim, God's messenger.

"These men have a whole world full of people who look at them with utter disgust. The father of a murdered girl once offered me ten thousand dollars to arrange for him to get into the cell with the man who killed his daughter. 'Just give me two minutes with him,' he begged me. That's the type of emotion people display around these inmates. They don't need yet another person who hates them, but they do need God. And my job was to act as His voice on earth. So, from that moment on, I've always done my best to switch off my personal feelings and allow the prisoners to talk with God, not me."

It wasn't always easy.

"There was one prisoner, a Hispanic guy, who came into the death house with such a cocky, bullish attitude. He didn't want help from anyone, didn't even want a cigarette or a last meal. This guy was just filled with rage. I asked him why he was so angry, and he said, 'Honestly, I'm not angry with no one. I'm just angry with myself. I did this crime.'"

That man was thirty-one-year-old Esequel Banda, who had broken into the home of an elderly housewife named Merle Laird when he was twenty-two.

"When someone wants to confess their crimes to me, it's my job to listen. He told me all about how he threatened and robbed her, then forced her to cook and serve him a meal. Once he finished eating, he raped and beat her. He then put on some music and ordered the poor woman to dance with him. As they were dancing, he drove a knife into her back, straight into one lung, and hugged her to him. When she started coughing up blood, he leaned in over her and sucked the blood from her mouth until she died."

Jim trails off and looks up at me. "Have you ever met pure evil?"

I once spent a weekend with the Ku Klux Klan while I was researching a piece about them. As we were eating blueberry pancakes and chatting about the coming race war, I started to feel a strange energy in the air around us. It really stressed me out, but I couldn't quite put my finger on it—not until I'd left, when my brother called to ask how it had gone, and I instinctively told him that it was like sitting at the kitchen table when we were kids.

He waits for me to go on.

The same familiar, unsettling sensation of being so close to uncertainty and danger. You can feel it in the air. You know you're sitting beside someone who could hurt you, someone unpredictable, and you know that at any moment, from one second to the next, everything could change—everyday life to danger in the blink of an eye.

I stop talking, thinking about the men who have scared me over the years.

I also spent some time in a courtroom in Norway, listening to a man calmly and matter-of-factly talk about how he killed seventy-seven people. That was incredibly unsettling, too. So yes, I think I've come close to pure evil a couple of times.

Jim Brazzil shakes his head and is quiet for a moment.
    "This man I was telling you about... his evil filled the room. That sort of brush with evil is something I only experienced a handful of times during my years as a chaplain on death row. The moment he died, I felt an overwhelming

sense of relief. I'm not ashamed to admit that. It was a good thing he had finally left this earth."

How did it feel when you sensed that kind of evil in the room?

"It made the hair on the back of my neck stand on end. I'm not easily frightened, but as he took his last breath, it was like a darkness spread through the room—a cloud that filled the space. And it wasn't the kind of cloud that rose; it was one that settled. I've only felt that way with a handful of people. At that moment, I knew he'd gone to Hell. I saw it happen."

What do you think Hell is like?

"In my mind, it's somewhere with a burning lake. There are demons, and there's suffering. It's not somewhere I want to visit, and it's not somewhere I even like to imagine."

I'm not sure I believe in Hell, but I've spent my entire life with a devil on my shoulder, whispering mean things to me. For a long time, it was alone there, but in recent years, it's been joined by a kind figure on my other shoulder, someone who whispers encouraging things instead. It's difficult to tip the balance in the right direction, though—to focus on the other figure rather than listening to the Devil.

. . .

"I guess that's the whole point of the Devil, whatever your opinion of him. He draws people in and tries to lure them toward him."

Who else were you convinced went straight to Hell?

"Juan Soria, Gary Graham, and Ponchai Wilkerson."

Only those four?

"Only those four."

Juan Soria had been sentenced to death for fatally stabbing another man in the head.

"I met him a few times, and he was a real nutjob. Back when he was on death row, there was a volunteer pastor who used to come in to see the inmates. The pastor wasn't a prison employee, but he was still given free access to death row, and he often chatted with Soria. One day, around three months before Soria's execution date, the pastor went up to his cell. The prisoner seemed to be acting like his usual self, and he said, 'Chaplain, you've been good to me. I appreciate everything you've done and want to make a bracelet for you. Can I do that?' The pastor said okay, and Soria said, 'I need to see how big your wrist is.' At the bottom of the doors, there was a gap just wide enough to push your hand through. He asked the pastor to do that, and the man got to his knees and did as he had been told. Soria then grabbed him. He pulled a razor blade from somewhere and slashed all the way around his arm, right down to the bone. There were scraps of flesh hanging off him, and he very nearly bled out.

"Fortunately, he survived. The prison staff managed to get him up to the hospital wing, where he was given a blood transfusion. He was later flown to Houston and spent several weeks in the hospital, but for a while, it was touch and go whether he would survive."

Did you know that pastor well?

"He was an acquaintance, but I wouldn't say I really knew him. I actually went to visit him in the hospital. He had a stroke while he was there and died six months later. He never really recovered. Soria was just looking for a new trial in an attempt to push back his execution date, but it didn't work. He went crazy when he realized it would go ahead as planned. They had to transfer him to the psychiatric unit in Houston, and that's where he stayed until the end. Because he was on the psych ward, his sisters were allowed to visit him on his last day. They wanted to say goodbye. He came in, and the guards put him in a cage. The man was drooling, slurring, and stuttering like crazy. I remember him sitting there with saliva hanging from his mouth, looking like he was high on something. His sisters broke down in tears, of course; they thought it was awful that someone so sick could be executed."

The afternoon wore on, and at around 4:30, his lawyer arrived.

"Juan Soria kept slurring and drooling with him, too. And then they took him back to his cell. At 5:00 or so, we got a call to say that his appeal had been denied and his execution would go ahead as planned. That was his last shot. I put the phone down, turned to him, and said, 'The court just rejected your appeal. The execution is going to take place." He looked back at me and said calmly and clearly, 'Well, it was worth a shot.' He'd been faking it the whole time."

The third person Jim is convinced went straight to Hell was Gary Graham.

He was only seventeen when he was arrested on May 21, 1981, following a 911 call from a female taxi driver. When the police got to the woman's hotel room, she told them that she had been kidnapped at gunpoint and raped repeatedly over the course of five hours. Graham had eventually fallen asleep, at which point she had managed to take his gun and call the cops.

When investigators began looking into crimes committed over the past week, they discovered—with the help of multiple eyewitnesses—that young Graham could be linked to twenty different robberies, ten stolen cars, and three attempted murders. He was also connected to a robbery-homicide that had taken place eight days earlier.

Gary Graham confessed to everything but the murder, and in his subsequent appeals, he claimed that he hadn't been given a fair trial, citing racism and prejudicial attitudes.

On the day of his execution, it took six men to carry him in from the prison transport vehicle. He shouted and fought against them all the way into the death house.

. . .

The final member of Jim's four, Ponchai Wilkerson, is the reason there is now a red sign on the last door before reaching the death row prisoners at the Polunsky Unit in Livingston, Texas.

The sign informs anyone entering the unit that the prison and its staff bear no responsibility for their life or safety and that, in the event of a hostage situation, they will not give in to any prisoner demands in order to secure a safe release. It was put up after a female guard was overpowered by two death row inmates, Ponchai Wilkerson and Howard Guidry, in February 2000. The two men wanted to bring attention to the condemned prisoners' living conditions by taking the woman as their hostage, and they demanded to meet the leaders of various human rights organizations in exchange for her release.

That evening, three men entered death row alongside the prison warden to discuss the prisoners' rights. The drama lasted thirteen hours before the guard was eventually released unharmed. Conditions at the prison improved, if minimally, but Ponchai Wilkerson was executed according to schedule three weeks later, and his death proved memorable to everyone present. As he lay on the gurney in the chamber, he spat out the key to a pair of handcuffs. No one knew where it had come from.

Did Ponchai Wilkerson and Gary Graham confess to you?

"No. They talked with me, but they didn't say anything about their crimes."

. . .

Ponchai Wilkerson had to be carried into the execution chamber, but was he calm while he was with you?

"He was calm. He talked to me. I was practically the only person he would talk to, not that it was a pleasant conversation. Everything about his face and his voice radiated evil. He saw everyone as the enemy and said as much to the guards that day. He told them, 'I'm going to fight you. I'm not going calmly. The only way I'm leaving this room is if you drag me out.'"

The same was true of Gary Graham. On the day of his execution, several famous activists, including the Reverend Al Sharpton, Jesse Jackson, Martin Luther King III, and Bianca Jagger, were present to offer support.

"I couldn't believe all these people were using him as the poster boy for abolishing the death penalty because he deserved to die. He was a terrible person to use to further their cause. The anger and rage that man carried... He played the race card, but as far as I could tell, it had nothing to do with the color of his skin. He was just a terrible person who'd done terrible things."

The staff kept Gary Graham on suicide watch around the clock, and in order to prevent him from harming himself or others, he was only permitted to wear a paper jumpsuit.

"Whenever he came in, he would shout and curse and spew bile at everyone, and whenever the guards were near, he would yell at them. It got to the stage where I had to ask them to stay away so we could talk.

"When the time came for him to die, Gary Graham kept his word about fighting until the very end.

"The team who came to get him that evening wore full protective uniforms. They opened the door and went straight for him. They hit him in the chest, making him fall back against the wall, and then they threw themselves on top of him. He was yelling like crazy, but it didn't take them much more than seven or eight seconds to pin him down, pick him up, and carry him out above their heads. I just stood there, watching the whole thing. And when I looked down, I saw four big clumps of his hair on the floor."

The guards put him down on the gurney and secured the straps.

"They'd called in an extra man that evening. The procedure was always to strap down the inmate's chest and feet, but with him, they also strapped his head down so he couldn't lift it. As they were struggling with him, they managed to tear his paper jumpsuit, meaning some of his body was visible. The warden made a quick decision to cover him with a sheet. Since that day, the prisoners have always been covered with a sheet during executions in Texas. We figured it was more practical that way."

It's also symbolic to pull a sheet over a person's face once they're dead.

"Right, and that was the pastor's job. Once they were declared dead and the doctor was gone, I covered them up. In Gary's case, I didn't pull the sheet up over his head because it wasn't... It was all new, something we hadn't done before. But after that, we did it every time—more out of respect for the relatives than anything, one last act of kindness."

In 1996, Janice finally announced that she wanted a divorce and she had never intended to move to Huntsville with Jim.

"I told her, 'If you want a divorce, you'll have to organize it. I don't want to get divorced. I want you. I love you."

She got herself a lawyer. Jim didn't contest the proceedings, but he didn't get behind them or hire a lawyer of his own.

Chapter Ten

They look me in the eye and confess to abusing children,
to rapes and murders, and I can't say a word to anyone.

1997

In 1997, Texas carried out thirty-seven executions—a record
at the time. More people were put to death in the state that
year than anywhere else in the civilized world, sometimes as
many as four a week. Twice during Jim's time as a prison
chaplain, he actually had to attend two executions in a row.

"Two in one night, that was tough. The judge sets the
date, and two different judges were involved. The first time
it happened, one of the prisoners was taken to the death
house while the other stayed behind at the Ellis Unit. The
first man was incredibly tense, beside himself with nerves.

They took his body away the minute he was dead. The second man had already been picked up by that point, and they just drove round and round in circles outside while they waited. Once the warden gave the sign, they pulled up, led him inside, and went through the usual procedures before saying, 'Okay, let's kill him.' I told them that I needed some time with him first, so they gave me a little while, maybe fifteen or twenty minutes, and then he went into the chamber and died. That was a strange night."

On June 4, 1997, Jim found himself facing another double execution when the state killed thirty-year-old Dorsie Lee Johnson-Bey Jr. and thirty-two-year-old Davis Losada.

"That was a really hard experience. I expected them to come in separately like the time before, but to my surprise, they brought the two men in together, one Mexican and one Black."

The inmates arrived around 1:00 p.m., and Jim spent some time running back and forth between the two, trying to talk to both of them.

"The first one was extremely remorseful and acknowledged what he had done. He knew he'd made mistakes, and he asked for forgiveness; he'd welcomed Christ into his life. He radiated peace and submission at the end, which meant he was very easy to deal with, but he was also afraid to die. The other man was very bitter. Hostile. There was something distant about him, and he wouldn't let anyone in. He was so angry—an angry man. I went back and forth between the two, doing my best to give them both time to talk. At first, the angry one wasn't interested at all. He said, 'Y'all are just cogs in the killing machine.' But the other guy said, 'Man, could you chill out? They're not doing anything we don't deserve.' Those were his exact words. And the other man replied, 'Speak for yourself.' He kept up that attitude, and in the end, the time came for the first of them to die. The warden came in, and the prisoner started crying when we told him, but he walked calmly by my side to the chamber. He hopped up onto the gurney and died very peacefully."

Everything said in the execution chamber is relayed over the speakers to the cells behind it, so Jim knew the other prisoner would have heard the whole thing.

"Once the first execution was over, I asked the warden if I could have a quick word with the second inmate. He said okay, and I went back through there. 'Man, that was horrible,' the prisoner groaned. I agreed, 'Yes, it's awful if you haven't made peace with God.' He didn't take that chance, but he did treat me with respect. We walked through to the chamber together, and he was executed just a few minutes later. That was a tough day, with one prisoner who was completely submissive and another who was obstinate. Having to deal with such polar opposites was hard work."

Two of Jim's children were living with him at the time, and he says that they could always tell whether the execution had gone well or not.

"As my kids explained it, sometimes I seemed like I was completely drained of all emotion when I got home. I was physically, spiritually, and mentally exhausted. They could tell right away when it had been tough."

One day, Jim felt utterly empty when he got back to the house. He quickly took off his work clothes, poured himself a glass of iced tea, and remembered that he had some leftover fried chicken from the night before. Right then, however, the phone rang. It was Larry from the public information office, who told him that a radio station in California wanted to interview Jim about the execution he had just attended. Jim agreed and sat down on the floor to chat with the reporter. His son, Brian, came into the house while they were talking, and he immediately started laughing harder than Jim had ever seen him laugh before.

"I was sitting there, doing my best to have a deep conversation about spiritual matters, and it really grated to see Brian carrying on like that. Once the interview was over and I'd gotten off the phone, I asked, 'What is wrong with you?' Brian was still laughing his head off, but he said, 'I'm never gonna get that image out of my head. You sitting on the floor with a chicken drumstick in one hand, a glass of iced tea beside you, wearing nothing but your red underpants, having a conversation about Jesus and executions.'"

Jim looked down and realized his son was right.

"That became a kind of in-joke between us. When I went to work ahead of another execution a few days later, Brian said, 'Don't forget to put your red underpants on!' Why not, I thought. And it... it became a kind of habit after that."

You started wearing red underpants to every execution?

"Yup. The same pair every time. They were pretty worn out by the end."

Thank you for that image I'll never get out of my head.

. . .

"You're very welcome."

The inmates... During all these executions in your red underpants, did you ever ask them: "Did you do it?"

"I never asked. I didn't need to. They told me themselves."

Of the 155 condemned prisoners you accompanied to the death chamber, how many talked to you about their crimes?

"I'd guess seventy-five percent."

And did any of them plead for their lives?

"No. Sometimes, they would ask not to be stuck with a needle. They would say, 'I'm scared of needles. Please, please, no needles.' But never anything about the fact they were going to be killed. They never used the word 'kill,' either. It was always just, 'Don't give me the needle.'"

The first time we met, you said that when Warner Brothers contacted you, they wanted to change a few parts of your story. They wanted you to plead with the governor to pardon a man, for example, and to have you save someone's life at the very last moment. Were those just things they made up, or did anything like that ever actually happen?

"I think I stopped a bloodbath once. The man scheduled to die was a Mexican citizen. I don't even know what he'd done —this was back when I still tried to keep out of their crimes— but whatever it was, it happened down in Brownsville. Anyway, because he was Mexican, the authorities there didn't want us to execute him. They said we didn't have the right. Stuff like that always happened when foreigners were involved. But this guy, he was furious. His mom was there, his wife, and he was just beside himself with rage. He was transferred to the prison, shouting, cursing, and acting up. I crossed the street to get the family ready for the execution, and his wife looked me in the eye and said, 'If he dies, blood will be spilled on the streets of Texas tonight. I've got people waiting down on the border; it'll be a bloody night.'"

What did you do?

"After we talked, I went straight to the prison warden. I told him what she had said, and he called Internal Affairs. He also got in touch with the police in Brownsville, and they temporarily closed the border between Texas and Mexico. No one could get in or out. The warden then sent me back to the prisoner, and the first thing he asked was, 'How's my wife doing?'"

Jim confronted the man and asked whether he was aware of his wife's plans for a bloodbath and whether he

138

really wanted to be responsible for a situation in which his wife ended up in prison purely to avenge his inevitable death.

The man lowered his head and said his friends wanted to avenge him.

"I said, 'So you think you're important enough for all these people to get hurt and suffer, maybe even die? Your son won't get to know either his mother or his father, and all because you want revenge? Why are you doing this?' And he replied, 'I'm not doing anything. You're killing me.' I said, 'It's not me killing you; you're killing yourself. You're guilty of the crime you're going to be executed for.'"

After a while, things calmed down. Jim told the man that he was the only one who could prevent the bloodbath, and the man seemed to be thinking, so Jim suggested that he write a letter to his wife. He promised he would deliver it to her.

"He started pacing back and forth in his cell. He walked over to the toilet, spat into it, turned back, and then said, 'Give me a pen and some paper.' I did as he asked, and he wrote a letter in Spanish to his wife."

Jim headed back up to the warden's office, and on his way there, he bumped into his colleague Joe Guzman, a Spanish-speaking guard who would be one of the members of the restraint team at the execution. He asked him to tag along and translate the letter for them.

"It said exactly what I'd been hoping it would, 'Too many people will get hurt; there's been enough bloodshed already. Let's just stop this. Call it off and keep things calm tonight. You know I love you, so let this be the last good deed I ever do.'"

The warden ordered Jim to take the letter to the woman

but to do so surrounded by the four burliest guards in the prison.

"She was still furious when I arrived, but I eventually got her to sit down and held the letter out to her. I said that her husband had asked me to give it to her, that it was a letter to her, and that he had chosen to write it. She read the whole thing, and then she lowered the paper to her knee. She looked up at me and didn't say a word, then looked down and picked it up again. Her hand was shaking, and she broke down in tears. I didn't reach out to comfort her; I just left her to cry for a few minutes. At that point, I did touch her hand. I said, 'You have the power to stop this,' and she nodded."

Jim asked the woman if she wanted to borrow a phone. She said yes, and the Spanish-speaking guard came in to supervise the call. She phoned two people.

"I don't know who they were; I have no idea, but no blood was shed that night. There was no violence. Everything went smoothly. But the man, the Mexican, I knew it was over for him, that he'd never get to Heaven no matter how much I talked to him. We might have stopped a bloodbath, but I didn't help him find peace; there was no peace to be found outside of Christ."

Jim pauses and leans back in his seat.

"As for whether I ever saved anyone at the last minute... No, but it nearly happened once. I was speaking with a death row prisoner from Wichita Falls. He'd killed someone there, but he kept on insisting he was innocent until the day of his execution. Once the inmates are taken to the death house, they're allowed to make a few calls—depending on their behavior—and we used to let some of them talk for a long time. That's not common knowledge, but it's true. This particular guy called his uncle to say goodbye. I think his uncle lived in Wichita Falls, too, and he told him that someone had come forward with new evidence that would prove his innocence. After the call, the inmate got all worked up. He said, 'I need to get out of here. I can prove I'm innocent.' I asked him to tell me what he knew and said I would see what I could do. I didn't believe him, but I felt like I had to pass the information on in case there was something to what he was saying, so I went to talk to the warden. This was around 3:00 in the afternoon."

Jim recapped what the prisoner had said and described how his demeanor had changed after the phone call. The warden called the governor's office and was asked to temporarily stay the execution while they looked into it, but just a couple of hours later, they called back.

"They said, 'We can't find any proof of what he's claiming. We talked to everybody, and there's no new evidence.' So, he was executed as planned."

That left Jim with a nagging sense of doubt. Was the man innocent after all? On the other hand, why the sudden change in personality if he wasn't guilty?

"After that call, he basically stopped talking to me, and that made it difficult to prepare him for what lay ahead. In the end, he calmed down, and he actually thanked me for what I'd done. He knew I tried."

Did you ever see anyone you believed to be innocent die?

"Yes, I did. His name was Benjamin Boyle—a quiet, older man from Oklahoma. He didn't have the same sort of attitude as the others."

Jim got to know Boyle at the Ellis Unit. He was open and polite, and on the day of his execution, he said, "I didn't do this, but I'm going to tell you my story."

"He told me he was a truck driver and that he and his wife were getting a divorce. Things were really bad between them, so he started selling drugs to give her a decent sum of money and buy himself a new truck. That was what he wanted. He was a long-hauler, and he stopped off in cities along the way to sell drugs."

On the way to Amarillo, he had—by his own account— around half a million dollars in cash and at least the same amount worth of drugs in his truck. From what he earned on that drive, he could give his wife whatever she needed and then head out onto the road for good.

"He picked up a girl along the way. She said, 'I'll let you do whatever you want with me so long as I can use your truck while you're gone.' Boyle agreed, and they had sex before he headed out to sell his drugs. He was gone for around two hours, and by the time he got back, he needed to get going pretty quickly, so he got into the cab, realized it was empty, and assumed that the woman must have left. He pulled out onto the highway, decided he wanted a cigarette, and got his hand caught on something when he reached back for the pack. He turned around, and there she was."

In his confession to Jim, Benjamin Boyle explained that he slammed on the brakes and skidded, hit a culvert, and managed to blow two tires. There he was, with a million dollars in cash and a dead woman in his cab.

"His immediate thought was, 'I'm dead either way. If the cops don't kill me, the drug dealers will.'"

Boyle wrapped the woman in a sheet, which he secured with duct tape—leaving his fingerprints in the process. He then hid her body in a culvert, called for a mechanic to fix his tires, and went on his way.

"It didn't take long for them to find her. The cops already had his prints on file, and I think they arrested him for murder two days later. He told me, 'I didn't kill her. I never fought the charge, never fought it at all, but that's because I've done way worse. I'm only getting what I deserve.' That was all he said about it, but he was a nice guy to talk to. He really was."

The official version of events differs from Benjamin Boyle's last confession in several ways.

His victim was Gail Smith, a twenty-year-old woman who worked as a waitress, not a prostitute. She was saving up for a car, but at the time of her death, she often hitchhiked to visit her mom in Lake Meredith, hundreds of miles away. On the day in question, a friend saw her getting into a large red truck marked Ruger Freight. The investigators managed to trace the firm back to Oklahoma, and on examining the schedule, they discovered that Benjamin Boyle was the only driver in the area on that particular day.

When the police searched his truck, they found a roll of silver tape and several sheets and blankets. Fibers from the latter were sent to the FBI in Washington, and it was quickly established that they were identical to the fibers found on Gail Smith's body.

A background check revealed that Benjamin Boyle had attempted to kidnap a twenty-eight-year-old woman in Colorado Springs in 1979, but she had managed to stab him and escape. Boyle was arrested, and after pleading guilty, he was sentenced to five years of probation. At the time of his arrest in Texas, he was also wanted for a different rape in Colorado after the victim identified him from a photograph. When the police continued to investigate his trucking route, they managed to link him to another homicide in California, where an unidentified body had been found on June 21, 1985. The woman's naked body had been shoved into a cardboard box, her hands and feet bound with tape.

"On the evening of his execution, both his brothers came to the prison. They lived in Dallas. I think one was a dentist, and the other a car salesman. They were good people, and I talked to them and prepared them for his death. They had already lost their last chance at an appeal."

Once it was all over, Jim took the man's belongings to his brothers and asked if they would like to eat dinner with him at Texan Café, a Huntsville institution on the other side of the street from the Walls Unit.

"It was late evening by then—this was after we moved the execution time from midnight to 6:00 p.m. The sun had set, but it was still pretty light out. You know, that eerie time of day. I don't know if you find it eerie or not, but I've always thought of it as an odd time. And sitting there with those men... Their brother just died, but neither of them shed a tear. We really talked about him, and there was no anger there. It was simply a fact that their brother was gone."

Jim couldn't tell them what Boyle had said.

Did you ever break your duty of confidentiality?

"I'm breaking it now. This is the first time I've ever talked about these things. I never told anyone, and that was really hard at times—really, really hard."

. . .

What made you decide to put your faith in me?

"Well, because you seemed honest, you weren't judgmental."

I'm probably a little judgmental. Some of the things you've said have made me bristle.

"Yes, but I knew you were coming here with a different attitude and a different outlook. That didn't matter because you let me speak from the heart. You seemed different. This isn't just about writing a bestseller. You're not out to trick me or prove me wrong; you're just exploring my story. With all the media folks I've encountered in the past, it always went something along the lines of, 'How can you be such an awful person and help with all these executions?' They wanted to twist it into some kind of political statement, but that's not for me. I don't care about politics; I care about the people involved."

Was there ever a time when you desperately wanted to break your duty of confidentiality?

"There was a kid in Dallas. He's probably the reason I ultimately decided to tell these stories."

The young man in question had robbed a convenience

store and killed a person, and was caught by the cops within just a few hours.

"After he was arrested, the police took him to Dallas County Jail, and he called his dad to say that he was in trouble."

His father told him not to worry, that he would send a lawyer, and that he just had to do what the lawyer said.

"That same morning, the lawyer marched into the room, put his briefcase down on the table, looked the kid in the eye, and said, 'Listen to me now. If you're guilty, I don't want to know; don't tell anyone. Never confess out loud because if you do, someone will hear it, and they'll put you to death. Never confess.'"

The lawyer left, and a few hours later, the boy's father visited him in jail.

"He looked his son in the eye and said, 'I'll only ask you this once, and I'm going to trust that you wouldn't lie to your own father. Did you do it?' And the son held his eye and said, 'No, Dad. I'm innocent.'"

The father believed his son and was heartbroken that his boy was being wrongly held for murder. He took out another mortgage on the house to pay the lawyer's fees, drew on his pension, and used all the family savings to give him the best possible defense. But despite all that, his son was still sentenced to death.

"The whole thing was so stressful that the father ended up dying of a heart attack. When the kid—now a man—told me this story, he spoke about how his mom would have to be there in the death house to watch him die. He said, 'As I'm lying on that gurney, I'll look her in the eye. She's lost everything, absolutely everything. I need to die with her thinking I'm an innocent man, but I can't set foot in that room without having confessed at least once. I did it. I'm guilty.'"

Jim tells me that he prayed with that man for forgiveness before he accompanied him into the execution chamber. Sure enough, as the condemned man's mother gazed through to him from the witness room, he said that he was innocent. And then he was executed.

"I went over to the Hospitality House to meet with her and give her his possessions later, and she was just so angry— really full of hate. They took her poor boy from her, and she was furious. She said, 'I lost my husband, and now I've lost my innocent son. It's not right. The state of Texas is awful.' And so on. It took all my strength not to tell her the truth."

Jim concedes that she probably wouldn't have believed him even if he had.

"I really don't think so. She would have just said I was trying to make him look bad. No matter what I did, it would have been wrong. It was a real lose-lose situation."

Jim has met the man's mother several times since the execution, and she still has no idea that her son confessed to his crimes before he died.

Until now, that was something only Jim Brazzil knew... Jim and God. He told me that it was a heavy burden to carry.

"Needless to say, it's incredibly hard sometimes. Even the executioner has a sidekick in there, an assistant, in case something goes wrong. But I had no one. These men, they look me in the eye and confess to abusing children, to rapes and murders, and I can't say a word to anyone.

Chapter Eleven

I think a person has to forgive in order to live their own best life.

1998

On February 3, 1998, Karla Faye Tucker became the first woman to be executed in the United States since 1984, when Velma Barfield was put to death in North Carolina. She also became the first woman to be executed in Texas since Chipita Rodriguez was hanged in 1863 during the American Civil War.

Karla Faye Tucker was beautiful, relatively young—just thirty-eight—and a born-again Christian. The case provoked a huge uproar, leading to headlines all over the world. Pope John Paul II wrote a letter pleading with the authorities for her life to be spared, as did several famous TV preachers and the World Council of Churches—even the brother of one of her victims. Thousands of people gathered in protest outside the Walls Unit, and they were joined by countless TV crews.

Jim Brazzil calls it a circus and tells me that some twenty male prisoners, both on death row and in regular prisons, offered to take her place in the chamber so that Karla Faye could live. The execution garnered so much attention that the authorities ultimately made the decision to fly her to Huntsville.

"It takes three hours to drive here from Gatesville, so they determined that from a security point of view, it was best to fly her over the night before."

Jim met her at the Goree Unit, a transitional facility that was once a women's prison. When the unit became too small, the majority of the inmates were moved to Gatesville, but Goree is still used to house women awaiting execution because of the facilities there. At that unit, her family was allowed to visit her. Karla Faye Tucker had fallen in love with a preacher during her incarceration and ended up marrying him.

"The media always called him a prison chaplain, but he wasn't. He was a volunteer. Still, he was a nice guy. I can't say whether it's true or not, but rumor has it that the guards organized the wedding and let them enjoy their ceremony together. They were allowed to hug and kiss each other. Death row prisoners aren't usually allowed to touch anyone, but I heard it was a real wedding and that they got to consummate the marriage in her cell."

. . .

149

Before Karla Faye arrived at the death house, the whole area had been cordoned off and barricaded so that no one would be able to drive up to the building. She was taken over there in a big Caprice, the regional director's own personal car, which had tinted windows.

"You couldn't see through any side windows or the rear windshield. A white van might have attracted attention, maybe even protests, so they used that anonymous car instead."

When she arrived, they opened the door, and she stood up.

"The wind caught her beautiful curly hair. It danced in the wind as if it knew that it was never going to dance again."

Karla Faye Tucker was twenty-three when she and her then-boyfriend murdered two people with a pickaxe during a burglary.

"The purpose of the death penalty is to prevent criminals from re-offending, and I have no doubt at all that if the Karla Faye Tucker who was arrested had been set free, she would have killed again. But the Karla Faye Tucker I met on death row fifteen years later? That's a different matter."

Jim tells me she was in a good mood ahead of her execution.

"She said, 'Send me home. I know where I'm going. If they give me a stay, don't tell me.'"

Karla Faye and Jim had actually become good friends during her years as a prisoner, and they spent a while praying together and chatting.

"She was very nice. The same goes for her sister and her husband; they were all nice people. I was about to go to the

150

Hospitality House to talk to her family, and she asked if she could hold onto my Bible to read while I was gone. I said yes and held it out to her without giving it another thought. By the time I got back, we had to head to the chamber. She was very easy to deal with—no problems at all. I actually have a photograph of her making her way into the chamber that day."

You still have it?

"Yes. I'm not supposed to, but I do. There was a guy called Chuck Bruce who used to come to the prison to take pictures during noteworthy executions and that kind of thing."

How many of these photographs do you have? That you're not supposed to, I mean.

"I have two."

Why did you want a picture of Karla Faye Tucker making her way into the execution chamber?

"Because it was such a high-profile event and because she left a lasting impression on me. She died with dignity, and I really mean that. I believe her faith was genuine. I believe that God had come to her and that He had changed her life, allowing her to give herself over to Him. She was so peaceful during the whole process."

Why did she leave such an impression on you?

"Probably because of her faith and because she was the first woman. You never really think that women can be executed, especially not back then. No other woman had been executed here in over a century. It took a lot from all of us to be able to do it. Once it was all over, the warden, the executioner, and two of the men on the restraint team actually resigned. I left the prison right after it happened and saw a Christian TV channel broadcasting live outside. As I passed, I heard the presenter say, 'I just talked with the pastor who was present for the execution, and he told me....' I stared at her because I'd never seen her before in my life—never mind speaking to her. If even Christian TV shows are willing to lie to their viewers? I went home and cried."

The next day, Jim sat down with his Bible. Karla Fay Tucker had asked him to officiate at her funeral, so he started flicking through the pages in search of a suitable passage. Before long, however, he discovered that she had left him a message.

Jim struggles to his feet. His legs are sore, but he goes to fetch his Bible all the same. It is a well-thumbed copy clad in pale leather, and sure enough, a neat greeting is written on one of the first pages.

. . .

Chaplain Jim,

THANKS for bringing Jesus's love and company into my life as I prepare to meet Him face to face. YOU, my adored brother, were handpicked by God because of the compassion in your heart for those walking this path. May God's grace and peace continue to shine upon you for the rest of your days!

I love you in Jesus's name.

Your sister, Karla Faye

Psalms 16:11

The passage she referenced urged the Lord not to leave her soul in Hell but to "show me the path of life. In your presence there is fullness of joy; in your right hand there are pleasures forevermore."

I ask Jim Brazzil whether that is true, whether Karla Faye Tucker ended up in Heaven, and he tells me he is convinced that is the case.

Who is the other person you have a picture of? You said there were two.

"Kenneth McDuff."

Why did you want his picture?

"Because I'd known of Kenneth McDuff all my life. While Chuck Bruce was taking pictures that day, I told him I wanted one, and he said okay. He came to my office with it in a brown envelope, tossed it onto my desk, and then we never said another word about it."

Jim felt close to Kenneth McDuff for several reasons. For one, he had grown up not far from him, and he knew several of his relatives.

"I didn't know him personally, but he was a cowboy—the mean kind of cowboy. Probably one of the cruelest men I ever came across. He was a sex addict, and he did drugs. And as for the crime that earned him the death penalty, he and another guy drove by three teenagers, pulled a pistol, and forced them into the trunk. They then drove them someplace out near Waco, dragged the girl out, and put six bullets into the two boys.

"The boys' names were Robert Brand and Mark Dunman. They were cousins, aged seventeen and fifteen, and the girl's name was Edna Louise Sullivan. She was sixteen, Robert's girlfriend.

"He did terrible things to her. He took her to an old gravel pit and ripped off all her clothes. He forced her down onto the ground and then put a broom handle over her throat, and started having sex with her. She fought back, so he got his buddy to stand on the handle while he kept at it. He seemed to get a kick out of seeing her struggle, and she died while he was still inside her. I found it really, really hard to deal with him. By the time we met, he looked so old and mean. I'll never forget that."

The photograph he has is the last picture ever taken of McDuff.

"Like I say, the high-ups don't know I have it. The warden does, though. In it, McDuff is still in his cell, wearing nothing but his underpants. He's looking up, and he seems very peaceful. He'd killed seven or eight people all in, but he doesn't look like a cruel killer; he knew he had reached the end of his life. His whole demeanor had changed."

What was his execution like?

"That was an interesting night. While we were still in the cell with him, the warden came in and explained everything. He asked McDuff what he wanted to happen to his body, and McDuff said the state could bury him. The warden then asked whether he had any questions, and McDuff said the same thing as everyone else, 'Can I get a cigarette?' At that, the warden asked whether he had a light, and McDuff said, 'Yes, Sir. I do.' I saw how surprised the warden was, but he told McDuff to show him."

Kenneth McDuff instructed the warden to check the bag of possessions from his cell. Inside was a clock made from matches.

"It was a big, beautiful thing, shaped like a house. He had really done a good job with it."

McDuff asked the warden to pass him the clock, and he opened a little compartment with a lighter inside.

"The warden said, 'Sure, you can have a cigarette.' That was their entire conversation, though we laughed about it later. The inmates are often extremely creative with where they hide their contraband."

Did he talk to you about his crimes?

155

. . .

"No, he didn't say a word about them. He was pleasant enough, though—very polite. We just spent a calm afternoon together. He told me he wasn't a religious man, and I said I wasn't going to force him to think about Jesus. He didn't show any remorse."

Once the execution was over, the state was responsible for organizing his funeral. His relatives attended.

"That was a tough one. It felt personal because I'd known who he was for so long. When you don't know a person, it's easier to talk more superficially about spiritual things, but when you really know a person's character—and how bad it is—it's hard to say anything positive."

Do you have a favorite execution—for want of a better word?

"Jonathan Nobles. The night he died was fantastic."

Jonathan Nobles was on death row for the rape and murder of two girls in Austin. Jim had spent several years forging a relationship with him, and Nobles had taken part in his *Experiencing God* class.

"I knew him pretty well. He was honest about the fact that he'd done a terrible thing when he killed those girls, and as his execution approached, the mother of one of his victims actually requested a mediation meeting. We made all the arrangements, and the two spent eight hours together. I was there. It was wonderful."

A mediation meeting is a process that takes at least six months to organize, often longer.

"The mediator talks with the prisoner, and then he talks with the victim, often a relative. He has various thoughts and questions, which he goes through with both sides. Only once the mediator is satisfied that everything feels okay and that both parties are ready will he agree to facilitate the meeting. That's when the paperwork starts. There are so many things for both people to sign."

Whenever Jim Brazzil took part in a mediation meeting, the victim would come to the prison the day before to take a look around. The staff would make sure the inmate was kept in their cell while they were shown the canteen, the hospital wing, and an empty cell, so that the visitor could get some sense of what the prisoners' life was like there.

"They tend to think a lot about that, the family and friends of the victims—how the prisoners really live there. The next day, the inmate—in this case, Jonathan Nobles—is given fresh clothes and taken to a quiet room in chains."

The woman who requested the dialogue meeting was the mother of one of the two girls he had killed, and she was already waiting when he came in. Nobles sat down on the other side of the table, directly opposite her, with the mediator to one side.

"He didn't immediately say anything to her; he wasn't allowed. He just sat down. They nodded to each other, and the mediator explained how the process worked."

The rules in these sessions are extremely strict. The victim speaks first, and they have the right to say whatever they want. They aren't allowed to stand up or hit the prisoner, but they are allowed to talk freely. After that, it's the inmate's turn, and the victim has to listen. They then alternate between themselves, and while one party is speaking, the other is meant to keep quiet. There are pens and paper on the table in case either of them wants to jot down their thoughts.

"The mother didn't hold back. She had basically lost the rest of her family because she couldn't get over the death of her daughter. She started drinking and taking drugs, and her other children decided they wanted nothing to do with her. The murder completely ruined her life. She told him all that, didn't beat around the bush at all; she really let loose on him."

As it happened, Jonathan Nobles had become a Catholic during his time in prison.

"He really got into it. I can't claim to fully understand the Catholic faith, but I do know that the Catholic priest and the deacon who volunteered at the Ellis Unit were always talking to him. The man even had a letter from the Pope."

To the Catholic church, Jonathan Nobles was a reformed man who had atoned for his sins. He was a believer who could be used by God. And he sat perfectly still and listened while the woman scolded him.

"When he finally opened his mouth, he calmly told her that he was guilty and that he was the one who had caused her so much pain. He said that he had hurt her, and he couldn't imagine what that must have been like. He took full responsibility for everything and told her just how sorry he was. He then cried, and she did the same. It really was an emotional moment."

Once Jonathan Nobles finished speaking, the mother had more to say.

"There was a lot of anger on her part for almost an hour."

But, Jim tells me, there was also a gradual change. Rather than needing their conversation to be mediated, the two really started talking to each other. The woman told

Jonathan Nobles that she had given her heart to Jesus and found peace.

"She said, 'I want you to know that I can and have forgiven you for what you did to my daughter and for ruining my life and my relationship with my other kids. I care about you. I care about the fact that you need to get to Heaven, that you need to open your heart to God.' And he replied, 'My heart is open.' It went on like that for hours, and once it was all over, she said she wanted to hug him and touched his hands."

She said she wanted to hug him? Her daughter's killer?

"Yes."

How did he react to that?

"He cried because he didn't think he deserved her forgiveness. It was an incredibly moving moment."

I have such a hard time wrapping my head around that— forgiving the person who killed your own child.

"I often say that justice is when you get what you deserve. Compassion is when you don't get what you deserve. And mercy is when you get something you don't deserve."

· · ·

What do you mean by that?

"I think a person has to forgive in order to live their own best life. You're not necessarily doing it for the other person, but for yourself, for your own heart."

But how does someone actually do that?

"You reach a point where you don't want to carry that anger around with you anymore, and in order to achieve peace in your heart, you have to forgive the other person. It's a process just like love; it takes time to love someone, and it takes time to forgive, but once you've come far enough that you can say the words 'I forgive you,' then you'll be liberating yourself as much as the person you're forgiving."

The dialogue meeting took place just a few days before the execution, and when Jim went to talk to Jonathan Nobles afterward, the inmate was so thankful that he had been given a chance to meet the woman.

"On the night of his execution, he told me he was willing to do anything to help her as a result of the pain he had caused. He was remorseful and knew he had hurt God. Our whole conversation was very emotionally charged and genuine. He'd spent the afternoon praying, and it was a very religious evening."

When the prison warden asked Jonathan Nobles whether he had any last words, he began by thanking everyone.

"He was completely at ease with the entire process. He addressed the mother he'd met in mediation and said hello to her. She said hello back, and then she started crying. He apologized to her and took full responsibility for his actions. He was in tears himself, and he said, 'I deserve to die.'"

Then, once the warden had given the sign to start the execution, Nobles began singing 'Silent Night.'

"Everyone was completely speechless; no one had expected that. I glanced over to the mother of the victim, and she seemed so peaceful as she gazed in at him."

Jim tells me that the condemned man had a good voice—strong and clear.

"If you want to know how long it takes for a person to die when they're given the lethal injection, he had time to sing 'Silent night, holy night. All is calm; all is bright. Round yon virgin, mother and,' before he spluttered on 'child.'"

Jim trails off and starts humming the tune.

"We could hear the drugs beginning to take effect a few words earlier, but it wasn't until he got to 'child' that it was really over."

Do you think of him whenever you hear 'Silent Night' now?

"Yes, every time. But it didn't ruin it for me. I think his song actually made me appreciate it even more. The sense of peace we all feel around Christmas, he felt it that evening. Whenever I hear that song, it makes me feel good."

. . .

Was it a holy night?

"I think it was. He was taken straight to the Catholic church after the execution. They left him on the gurney, draped a sheet over him, and let his parents in. His body was still warm, of course, and that was the first time they had been able to touch him in years. It was a very emotional moment when they hugged, kissed, and said goodbye to their son."

Have you spoken to the woman from the dialogue meeting since?

"Many times. She was so grateful. She told me that she'd had mixed feelings on the night of the execution because she missed her daughter and wanted to be angry. But when she thought about the mediation, she realized that the forgiveness she had given him was far more important. It was an incredibly meaningful evening for me, too. The whole process was. And she came out of it a stronger person. She accepted his apology, and she really meant what she said."

Is that why his was your favorite execution?

"Yes. The peace he felt was genuine peace. The faith he demonstrated to me was genuine faith, too, just like Karla Faye Tucker's."

Jim says there have been a few such occasions when the

condemned prisoner's last words really stuck out—when they didn't just reel off the same old things about being innocent or saying goodbye to their family.

"I remember one man, Earl Behringer. I'd been to see him several times on death row. He was a friendly guy—not at all the death row type, in my opinion. He was cleanshaven, very clean in general, with no tattoos. He was always accommodating and friendly. When they pulled up with him in the van, I remember feeling the same sadness I often did at that final journey, knowing that this man had been brought here to die. It upset me every time. I never did get used to that."

The van came to a halt, and the doors opened. Earl Behringer was wearing the usual hand and leg chains, and it was a bright, sunny June day.

"As he got out of the van, he looked up at the sky, took a deep breath, and said, 'It's a good day to die.' He had a smile on his lips as he headed inside."

I remember you telling me about him the first time we met. His words stayed with me—a good day to die. I've actually been thinking about using them for the title.

"It's a good title. They stayed with me, too."

When he was twenty-two, Earl Behringer killed two people, a man and a woman around his age. He shot both multiple times in the head, and then he stole the woman's purse and the man's wallet.

"In his final words, he said the same thing he had when he first arrived at the death house. He said, 'It's a good day to die. I walked in here like a man, and I'm leaving here like a man. I had a good life. I have known the love of a good woman, my wife. I have a good family. My grandmother is the pillar of the community. I love and cherish my friends and family. Thank you for your love.' He then turned to the victims' families and said, 'I'm sorry for the pain I caused you. If my death gives you any peace, so be it.' And he continued, 'I want my friends to know it is not the way to die, but I belong to Jesus Christ. I confess my sins. I have.' Those were his final words."

How did that make you feel?

"It made me think that every day is precious. Today is a good day to live, and today is also a good day to die. That became a kind of philosophy for me. Each day will be whatever I make of it. If I have a bad day, that's because I let it be a bad day. Even though I'm now dying, too, that's how I see it. I saw what Earl did, and he chose to make the last day of his life a positive one. It was a good day to die. I thought that was fantastic."

Thinking of it as a good day to die is beautiful. Would today be a good day to die?

"It would. But it's also a good day to live."

I agree. We're having a nice time here despite all the talk of death.

"Life is what you make of it. That's the truth. I met another guy—Lackey, I think he was called. He was an old cowboy, the tough type. You could tell just by looking at him that he'd been through a lot, that he'd seen things. He was a country man through and through. I remember sitting with him. We'd already prayed that afternoon, preparing him for death. He had just been served his last meal, and he asked if I listened to country music. I told him it was practically all anyone listened to in those parts, and he asked if I would do him a favor. He wanted me to call the local radio station and ask them to play "Blue Clear Sky" by George Strait. That was his favorite song, he said. He really loved it."

Jim went to the warden, who gave him a firm no.

"He said, 'Can you imagine the reaction if people found out that a man on death row got to request music on the radio? Never going to happen.' I went back through to apologize and break the news to Lackey, and he said, 'Hey, at least we tried.'"

The two men continued their meal, still listening to the radio. They had tuned it to KSAM, the local country station in Huntsville.

"I usually turned off the radio around fifteen minutes before the execution, once all the preparations got underway. But when I reached out to turn the dial, he said, 'Don't turn it off, please.' So, I left it on. I'm not quite sure of the time, but I think it was around three or four minutes to six when the host introduced the next track, 'Blue Clear Sky' by George Strait. They played that song, and the warden came through the door just as it finished. It was time. Lackey said, 'Wow, I couldn't have asked for much better than that.' It gave me such a warm feeling to know that his last request had been fulfilled after all. He went through to the execution chamber with a smile on his lips. That's how I want it to be for all of them. A good day to die."

Chapter Twelve

I knew what to say to men who were about to die,
but not to men who had been raped.

1998-1999

The inmate who arrived on August 11, 1999, immediately stood out from the rest. Both in terms of size—he weighed almost 400 pounds and had a fifty-six-inch waist—and hygiene.

"James Otto Earhart had a theory that if he never showered or washed his behind, no one would rape him in prison. The man stank something rotten. When he first arrived, the guards had to rinse him off with the fire hose."

Twelve years earlier, Earhart had kidnapped nine-year-old Kandy Kirtland as she walked home from school in

Bryan, Texas. Two weeks passed, and pictures of the brown-haired, blue-eyed girl went up all over town. On the fourteenth day, her body was found partially hidden beneath leaves and branches in a wooded area a few miles from her home. Her hands had been bound with cable ties, and an autopsy revealed that she had died as a result of a gunshot wound to the head caused by a .22 caliber pistol.

Earhart had gone to the Kirtland family home to look at a spray gun her father was selling a week before the girl vanished. The two men hadn't been able to agree on a price, but that was when Earhart saw the girl for the first time. A neighbor noticed the burly forty-four-year-old chatting to Kandy on the day of her disappearance and was able to give a detailed description to investigators. This led to his identification and arrest on the same day that her body was found. The police discovered articles about her case at his home, alongside literature about bondage sex. They also found a .22 caliber handgun in his car.

James Otto Earhart told investigators he had picked the girl up and driven around with her for a while before dropping her off, but he denied killing her. Traces of blood from his clothing proved to be a match for her blood type, however, and the rounds in his pistol corresponded with the bullet fragments found in her head. The prosecutor believed his motive for killing her was sexual, but her body was too badly decomposed for them to be able to tell whether or not she had been raped.

"Earhart spent years making one appeal after another, but they were all struck down. When he finally realized he was going to die, he confessed to both raping and killing the girl to me."

For once, Jim Brazzil did something unusual. He asked

the prisoner whether he could share what he had told him with the girl's mother, Jan Brown. Whether he could say that this really was the man who had killed her child, despite all his previous denials.

"I can't really explain why, but I just felt an urge to ask. And he said I could."

When James Otto Earhart was eventually strapped down on the gurney, he didn't say a word. Jim wasn't sure what to do, but since the prisoner had given him the go-ahead, he decided to tell the girl's mother he had confessed once the execution was over.

"It meant a lot to her to hear that. I wish more of the inmates had allowed me to share what they said once they were dead, even if they weren't willing to own up to it themselves."

Jim chose not to tell her that James Otto Earhart had also confessed to raping the girl.

"She didn't need to know that."

I've met Jan Brown. She told me that she described herself as "an opponent of the death penalty who benefitted from the death penalty." While she disagrees with the punishment in principle, she also couldn't help but breathe a sigh of relief when he died.

"That's a common feeling among relatives."

The fall of 1998 brought big changes, both for Jim and the inmates of the state of Texas.

On September 28, after two years of negotiation, Jim and Janice finally finalized their divorce. With that, twenty-seven years of marriage came to an end.

"We drove to the courthouse together, and the judge asked whether we really wanted to do this. She said yes, and I said no. And then it was done, and we went to IHOP and ate breakfast together. I had my usual order—pancakes, eggs, and bacon—but it felt like I had a lump in the pit of my stomach the whole time. It wasn't a good day. After the divorce, it felt like I was done as a preacher. Life was so lonely and empty. I was so... I never told anyone this before, but I was probably clinically depressed at the time. I went through a period where I easily could have driven off the road."

You thought about ending your life?

"Yes, I did."

Did you make plans?

"No. I wanted to. I wanted to die, but I had no intention of actually committing suicide. I knew that from day one. I was never going to go through with it, but I definitely fantasized about it."

. . .

It's a strange coincidence that we were just talking about Jan Brown. She told me how she planned to kill herself.

After her daughter's death, Jan Brown walked into a psychiatric clinic and told the staff there that she wanted to die. The doctor she saw asked whether she was thinking about ending her own life. She said yes, and the doctor asked *how* she was planning to go about it. Jan replied that she would drive her Cadillac into the garage, start the engine, turn the A/C on, and leave the engine running as she slipped away. He asked *when* she was planning to do it, and she said she would wait until the fall once her son had gone back to school. That way, he would be at his dad's place during the week, which meant he wouldn't be the one who found her. The doctor asked *who* she imagined might find her, and she explained that she was planning to write a letter to her friend, who was an attorney. The doctor asked her to describe that friend's reaction to finding her, and so she did. He then asked her to imagine herself lying in a coffin at the funeral parlor, to talk about how she looked and what the coffin was like. Jan described the type of flowers she envisioned on her coffin, and he asked her to take him through who would be present at her funeral. She did. He asked her to share what she thought those people might say, and then he asked what would happen to her body afterward—to tell him about the place where her coffin would be laid to rest. Again, Jan answered every question in great detail. And then the doctor asked her to imagine what it would be like to be in the ground, in the coffin as they filled in the grave above her.

As Jan Brown recounted this to me, she suddenly started laughing. It was a genuine laugh that felt completely out of place given the subject matter, though at the same time, it was also liberating. She told me how taken aback the doctor was, that he explained that he liked to do those thought exercises in order to work out just how serious a person was. The vast majority of patients couldn't even describe *how* they would end their own lives. Jan was the first person he had ever met who managed to answer all his questions.

She was admitted to the ward and remained there for a month. By the time I met her, she told me that she had slowly but surely managed to make her way back to some form of reality. A new reality in which her youngest daughter was dead, but she and her three other children were still alive—a reality in which, one day, she no would longer want to die.

Jim listens as I speak, thinking and shaking his head.

"No, I never reached that stage. I fantasized about driving straight into a rockface, but that's as far as I took it."

He pauses for a moment and sighs.

"My children were very important to me, and I felt like I'd failed them all by wrecking my marriage. That loss was just so palpable."

While Jim was battling his own demons, drastic changes were also underway on death row. Until 1998, all condemned prisoners in Texas were housed at the Ellis Unit, in their own wing, separate from the rest of the inmates. Within that limited environment, they were granted quite a lot of freedom. Those deemed trustworthy were allowed to work and, if they wished, to study. They had the right to several hours of group exercise and to watch TV, and the only time they were locked up alone was at night.

They were even, under certain circumstances, allowed visitors.

All of that changed over Thanksgiving 1998, when seven condemned prisoners attempted to break out. It was the first escape from a death row unit in Texas since 1934, when the infamous robber duo of Bonnie Parker and Clyde Barrow stormed into Eastham prison in Huntsville with guns drawn, killed two guards, and freed Clyde's cousin Raymond Hamilton.

The escape in 1998 wasn't quite so violent, but it was meticulously planned and carried out.

"The inmates had finished their meal—they were always given a special dinner on Thanksgiving—and were out in the yard. Because it was a holiday, the prison was fairly short-staffed.

"Seven of the prisoners had made dummies out of clothing and left them in their beds to trick the guards, and they then hid in the yard and waited for darkness to fall. Wrapped up in cardboard, newspaper, and several layers of clothing to protect themselves against the barbed wire, they made a run for the first fence, which they cut with a pair of hedging shears. They spent several hours hiding in the bigger yard, then they made a dash for the second fence, where they were spotted. The marksmen in the guard towers opened fire, and after around twenty shots were fired in rapid succession, six of the seven had thrown themselves to the ground and were eventually returned to their cells.

But one prisoner remained unaccounted for, and an unprecedented search was launched for twenty-nine-year-old Martin Gurule, who had been sentenced to death for killing a restaurant owner and chef in Corpus Christi in 1992. Some 500 police officers, dog patrols, and helicopters with thermal imaging cameras spent seven days searching for the escaped inmate, who was classified as "dangerous but unarmed." A reward of 5,000 dollars was also offered.

Jim describes what it was like to work in the prison that week. The atmosphere was tense, and the guards were all on edge. Everything was done by the book, and the prisoners themselves felt the pressure, being written up for even the most minor of infractions.

"It was like that everywhere, not just here but in prisons across Texas. Everyone suddenly started following the rules, and no one liked that. It was tough. The locals in Huntsville were terrified, too. They were all acutely aware that this prisoner had escaped and that he was a brutal, violent type. Wherever you went, there were guards. They called in teams from every prison from Palestine down to Houston, and they had people patrolling the streets, sitting in cars, watching and waiting, unsure of what might happen but fully conscious of the fact that there was a killer on the loose.

"But then, on the seventh day, Martin Gurule was found. Two prison guards had gone fishing on their day off, and one of them managed to reel in his dead body. He had been in the water for a week, and the wound on his back suggested he had been shot during the escape.

"I was still at the prison that evening, and the assistant warden came over to me and said, 'They found Gurule. Do you want to come?'"

Jim jumped into the car, and they drove out onto Highway 19.

"We were there when they pulled him out."

Although Gurule had been in the water for a week, his

body was still covered in newspapers and magazines, and Jim remembers seeing several pages from *National Geographic*.

"It wasn't a pretty sight. He'd been dead a long time, but it had also been cold, so his body wasn't in as bad a state as it might have been. I remember thinking about how scared everyone had been and that they could relax now. That was a relief because I knew just how stressed and nervous the guards were. The incident got so much attention that it made it hard for everyone, including the other prisoners."

The then-governor of Texas, George W. Bush, had ambitions of running for president, and he took a hard line. The fact that a death row inmate had managed to escape was unacceptable, and the residents of Huntsville had to be protected at any cost. As a result, rules were tightened, work programs at the Ellis Unit were canceled with immediate effect, and the decision was made to move all remaining death row inmates to the newer supermax prison in Livingston.

"They also fired a number of staff, of course—including the warden, who was a good friend of mine. The truth is that whenever something like that happens, someone is going to end up losing their job. It's never any of the real high-ups, though; it's always someone in a management position within the prison itself. That's how it goes. I think eight people lost their jobs after Gurule escaped."

Jim found the whole thing very unfair. He understood the rationale behind it but didn't think the staff deserved to lose their jobs.

"The warden wasn't even there the day of the escape, but they said he should have trained his staff better.

Someone will always be sacrificed in that sort of bureaucracy."

Over the next six or so months, death row was moved to the Terrell Unit, some 50 miles away.

"It was a huge change. At Ellis, the death row prisoners were kept away from the rest of the facility, but they were also able to work, go outside, talk, laugh, and watch TV with the others. Everyone did a trade of some kind, and they were allowed to make things in their cells. They had razor blades, and they had wood and matchsticks. They made boats and clocks and all kinds of objects... Crosses, so many crosses. Everyone was always making something. But all that was taken from them once they got to the new prison."

The Terrell Unit was named after Charles Terrell, the former chair of the Texas Department of Corrections. In 1999, when the facility first began housing death row inmates, Terrell got cold feet and asked the authorities to change its name. As a result, it became known as the Allen B. Polunsky Unit, after a former chair of the Texas Board of Criminal Justice—one who had no problem being associated with condemned prisoners. Since then, the Polunsky Unit has had the dubious honor of being named the worst prison in America on multiple occasions. It looks exactly how you might imagine a facility housing prisoners awaiting death might look: cold, spartan, and threatening.

The Polunsky Unit is made up of twenty-three drab, block-like buildings spread across an area of 584,000 square feet, surrounded by high walls, razor wire fences, and four guard towers manned by snipers with rifles. The guards in the four towers are authorized to use lethal force on anyone who sets foot on the thirty-foot strip of grass separating the parking lot from the wall.

Building 12, a two-story structure containing 290 cells, is where the death row inmates are housed. The cells in the Allen B. Polunsky Unit are small, under sixty square feet in size, and they are sparsely furnished with bare concrete floors. The walls are painted white, though they haven't been freshened up in a long time, and there is a small slit window made from reinforced glass around eight feet up from the floor. These windows, allowing a chink of daylight into the cells, are roughly four feet long but less than four inches wide. Still, if a prisoner climbs onto his bed and pulls himself up, he might be able to catch a glimpse of the sky outside. The beds themselves are around thirty inches wide, with thin, pale blue plastic mattresses. Beneath the bedframe are three compartments that can be used for storage, and beside the bed is a small wall-mounted shelf that also serves as a table. Prisoners aren't permitted a chair, which means they simply have to sit on their bed and lean forward. Above the little shelf/table, there is another narrow shelf screwed to the wall, and beyond that, there is a steel toilet without a seat.

The white cell doors have two tall windows with black mesh over the glass, plus a so-called bean slot. Before a prisoner leaves their cell, they have to kneel with their back to the door and push their hands out through this slot to enable the guards outside to cuff them. This means that some older inmates struggle ever to leave their cells because many long-term prisoners suffer from rheumatoid arthritis.

Death row inmates spend much of their time alone in their cells—in order for it to count as solitary confinement, a person has to spend at least twenty-two hours a day in isolation—but they have the right to two hours' recreation in a "dayroom," i.e., another, larger cage, five days a week. The prisoners never know when they will be given their recreation time; that is at the guards' discretion, and it varies from one day to the next for security reasons. The "dayroom" is located at the very heart of the building, meaning all the other prisoners can see it from their cells through the two windows in their doors. Each inmate is given the cage to themselves for two hours—even here, they are kept apart— and it is only while they are in the "dayroom" that they are able to talk to anyone but their immediate neighbors. There is also an outdoor cage, though this is used less often in Texas. In other states where the death penalty is in force, such as Connecticut, Ohio, and Tennessee, inmates are permitted an hour outside five days a week, weather permitting.

What do you think it meant for the prisoners' mental well-being to be able to do the things they were permitted to at Ellis, compared with life in the Polunsky Unit?

"It gave them something to focus on, so they weren't just sitting in their cells all day with nothing to do. It gave them purpose, direction, a sense of being, and community, even if it was just with the other inmates. Visiting death row at the Polunsky Unit now, there's none of that. Everyone is isolated. There's an old saying that if you treat a man like an animal, he'll behave like one, and it's true. The only real contact they have with other people is when the guards take them from their cells to the showers or the visitors' room."

A supermax facility like the Polunsky Unit has the

highest level of security in the U.S. prison system. The purpose is to enable the long-term segregated detention of prisoners classified as particularly high risk, those who pose a severe threat to national or international security.

Alcatraz, on an island of the same name just off San Francisco, has long been considered the prototype and early gold standard for a supermax prison. A large, nationwide drive to build supermax facilities was launched in 1983 after two correctional officers—Merle Clutts and Robert Hoffman —were stabbed to death by inmates in Marion, Illinois, and the Polunsky Unit is now one of over fifty such prisons spread across dozens of states.

Compared to regular high-security prisons, supermax facilities cost roughly three times as much. The higher costs largely stem from the technology required to operate the unit: the security doors, reinforced walls, and advanced electronic systems. More staff is also needed to keep all these things running.

Jim has mixed feelings about this development.

"I think supermax prisons are an effective way of managing the most dangerous inmates, but from a purely humanitarian point of view, I wouldn't want to live the rest of my life like that."

He used to travel over to the Polunsky Unit to talk to the death row prisoners every week, sometimes even two or three times.

"I remember heading over there once when one of the men was due to be executed. He was in his cell, and he refused to come out. When they opened the door, he huddled up in the corner of his bed, so they sprayed him with pepper spray. All the guards were wearing protective masks, but I wasn't. I remember trying to keep a straight face as the other prisoners started shouting and cursing at the guards. They were all on his side, as you can imagine. They knew he was about to die, so they wanted to give him their support by yelling as much as they could. It was so hot in there, and the pepper spray started to do its thing. His eyes were streaming, and his nose was running, but in the end, he came out. I remember just how much of a relief it was to walk away from the cell and get out into the fresh air that day."

You've met death row prisoners at the Ellis Unit, and you've met death row prisoners at Polunsky. What would you say was the main difference?

"I don't think the men in Polunsky see themselves as human anymore. They've had so much of normal life snatched away from them. I remember turning to a man as we prayed ahead of his execution and telling him, 'You can hold my hand if you like.' He looked up at me and said, 'That's the first time in sixteen years anyone has touched me.' That meant a lot."

Do you think it serves its purpose? In your opinion, should things be done like they are at Polunsky or Ellis?

"When it's done right, I prefer the Ellis approach. But the inmates there had way too much time on their hands. If the authorities could work out how to structure it differently, I think it would be better. On the other hand, there were more inmates killed by other inmates there."

Violence between prisoners is a big and growing problem in American correctional facilities. Around the year 2000, while Jim was still working within the system, an average of 40 inmates a year were killed by fellow prisoners. By 2018, that figure had risen to an average of 120 murders a year—though this data relates to regular prisons, where the inmates are able to interact with one another, not supermax facilities, where people are kept in complete isolation—something which, according to Amnesty International, is torture.

At the Ellis Unit, the prisoners were able to be in physical contact with one another, which meant they could have both consensual sex and rape one another.

"That's right, and it happened all the time. Rape is very common within prisons. Many of the men I met in the hospital wing had been raped, but they refused to say a word about it. They were afraid I would tell someone who attacked them, which could wind up getting them killed, so in that respect, they never trusted me. That was a group of inmates I wasn't able to give the help they deserved, unfortunately."

He trails off and thinks for a moment.

"That's actually true of male inmates and the women in mediation who'd been through the same thing. I just didn't know what to say to comfort them; I was way outside my comfort zone. I knew what to say to a man who was about to die but not to a man who had been raped."

Chapter Thirteen

*As time passes, with all the appeals and debates around the
death penalty, they start to think of themselves as victims.*

1999

Not long after his divorce, Jim Brazzil met Bobbie Blount, a
mother of two. She worked for the Public Information Office
at the Texas Department of Criminal Justice, preparing the
press packs distributed to the media before every execution.
These packs contained information about the perpetrator
and their crimes, including details such as the condemned
prisoner's weight upon arrival on death row and what he or
she weighed on execution day.

"At first, we were just friends. I went over there every
week because her boss, Larry, was a buddy of mine. He and I

would go to a Mexican place called Cinco de Mayo after almost every execution, and he would drink alcohol while I stuck to coffee or tea."

Bobbie joined them a few times, but their relationship remained platonic. She lived in Spring, Texas, with her two daughters, and, like Jim, she was divorced.

"I really liked her. She was a beautiful woman and funny. Bobbie was always laughing, and I needed that. She didn't have a bad word to say about anything. We became a couple toward the end of 1999."

Back on death row, serial killer Danny Lee Barber was one of the last inmates to be executed before the move from Ellis to the Polunsky Unit. He had been sentenced to death for the rape and murder of a woman in October 1979. During police interviews following his arrest, he also confessed to having killed another three people in the Dallas area over a two-year period.

"Danny was a chatty guy; he talked a lot. He was a dumb old redneck, an uneducated man. I know that doesn't sound very nice, but he was. I really did feel sorry for him throughout the whole process because he was so scared of dying."

The official execution time of 6:00 p.m. had come and gone that evening, but nothing is ever done until the courts have given the green light. As a result, it wasn't unusual to have to wait hours to hear from them.

"He was so tense, pacing back and forth. And once 6:00 passed, it got even worse. I really did have to work hard with these men when the process dragged out."

. . .

What did you do?

"Just talked and talked. But the more we talked, the worse things got. In the end, we reached a point where he was on the verge of some kind of breakdown, and that's when they called to say that he'd been granted a stay."

Jim turned to the prisoner and told him that he wouldn't be dying that evening. At first, Danny Lee Barber thought he was joking, but once he realized that the chaplain was telling the truth, that he really had been granted a stay of execution, he grew cocky.

"It was the way he said it that really stuck in my mind. 'I knew you guys wouldn't get me. You'll never get me.' That made me think he had no idea what went on inside those walls. Because the truth is that no one there wanted anyone to die."

Ten days later, Danny Lee Barber was given a new execution date in two months.

"The men on death row are convinced they're going to go through all sorts of horrible things when they get to the death house. They think they're going to poop and piss themselves, that they'll be forced to wear diapers, that they'll be prodded and beaten and abused. There are all sorts of rumors on death row, and unfortunately, some of the staff like to frighten the prisoners. If an inmate snaps up a piece of information, it spreads like wildfire, which means they're frightened before they even get to the death house. And since most people who head over there wind up dying, very few of them ever get a chance to come back and quash the rumors. Still, I think it's probably hardest for those who've been taken over there once before. They come to the death house, and they're treated with respect. No one hits them, and they're given the best food they've had since they wound up in prison. And then they're granted a reprieve and sent back to their cell, and they realize they'll have to go through the whole thing all over again—only next time, they'll die. It's tough on them."

When Danny Lee Barber arrived at the death house for the second time, he was a different man. Very quiet.

"He was actually given two stays of execution. Word of the second one came through before 6:00, but after that, it wasn't long before he was back again. I never saw him act all cocky again, though; he knew it wouldn't last forever. When he arrived for the third time, he actually said, 'I know this is the end.' The unusual thing was that he got three last meals. He ordered two steaks, a baked potato, salad, tea, chocolate ice cream, and cigarettes every time."

Prisoners' last meals are often a story in and of themselves, and some inmates come up with highly unusual requests.

"I don't think I told you this, but I met a guy from Fort Worth once. I don't remember his name, but he was a tall, skinny Black man. He was middle-aged, and you could see he'd been through a lot. In any case, I went over to the death house to meet him and find out what he wanted for his last meal. He asked whether he could order anything, and I said he could certainly try. And then he said, 'Well, I'd really love some chitlins.'"

Chitlins, or chitterlings as they are known outside of the Southern U.S., are part of the soul food tradition. The dish is made from the small intestines of pigs, carefully cleaned and

185

rinsed several times before being boiled for hours. Chefs often add a halved onion to the pot to counteract the strong aroma, which can be particularly powerful when the offal first starts to cook. Chitlins are sometimes dipped in batter and fried after boiling, and they are generally served with apple cider vinegar and hot sauce.

"It stinks. You start boiling the intestines, and it smells awful—like pig manure. It feels like you're actually in a pigsty. Still, the dish is very common among the Black community around here; they love it. The old folks like boiled chitlins, but the younger generation prefers them fried because they don't have the same unpleasant aroma. They pour hot sauce over them and wolf them down. I've never tried them myself and have no plans to do so, but I went to the warden that day and asked whether I could arrange something special for this inmate. The warden asked me what, and I said, 'Chitlins.' At that, he pulled a face and said they were disgusting."

The warden asked Jim how he planned to get hold of the dish, and the chaplain replied that he had been hoping one of the women who worked in the prison might be able to help. As long as Jim could fix it, the warden said he was welcome to give it a try.

"So, I went to the chapel and asked my assistant Lisa whether she had ever made chitlins before. She crinkled her nose and said she had, that they had stunk out her house."

Jim told her about his dilemma, and she shrugged and said okay. Lisa then went home to make a portion of chitlins and was back in time for dinner. Jim sent the dish down to the canteen, where the staff heated them up for him.

"When they took them to the prisoner, you almost could have thought it was Christmas. The joy on his face, the fact that he'd gotten what he wanted for his last meal. He asked me if I wanted a bite, but I just smiled and said no. I could barely stand to be in the room; it stank for two days afterward. But he enjoyed it. He ate every last bit, and that made all the difference to him."

Most states where capital punishment is in force offer inmates a final meal, but each has its own rules. For example, in Florida, the food must be purchased locally and cannot cost more than forty dollars. In Oklahoma, the limit stood at fifteen dollars for a long time, but has recently become more generous. When Donald Grant was executed there in January 2022, he enjoyed one of the most luxurious last meals the state has ever provided. He requested—and was served—sesame chicken, six egg rolls, shrimp fried rice, and a large apple fritter. In Louisiana, tradition has it that the warden joins the prisoner for their last meal as an act of courtesy. And in Ohio, where executions take place at ten in the morning, inmates eat their final meal the night before.

In 2011, Texas stopped offering death row prisoners a choice of last meal. Instead, inmates are given the same food as everyone else that day. The reason for this is that Lawrence Russell Brewer, a murderer and white supremacist, requested an enormous last meal and then refused to eat a single bite. That led the senator, John Whitmire, to put a stop to the eighty-seven-year-old tradition of letting condemned prisoners choose their final meal. However, during Jim Brazzil's time as a chaplain, the staff still did their best to give the prisoners what they wanted.

"Karla Faye Tucker wanted fresh fruit. She said she had been dreaming of a ripe banana, so I went to Kroger's and bought bananas and a peach for her. She cried as she ate that banana."

When I met Vaughn Ross, the death row inmate who led me to you, he must have spent at least seven minutes talking about an apple—about how much he missed them. The juice, the crunch when you take a bite. He went through every single detail.

"There's no fruit in prison. It's a real shame."

Jim often bought other items for the condemned prisoners, too.

"I bought a liver once. A guy wanted mashed potatoes, liver, and onions for dinner. Another time, an inmate wanted a malt shake. For a while, I felt like I might wind up broke because I was paying for everything out of my own pocket, and this was back when there were a lot of executions. They always requested something, and I wanted to feel like I was making a difference in their lives. By giving the prisoners something they really wanted, I felt like I could do that."

Jim tells me that it wasn't just out of the goodness of his own heart. It was tactical, too.

"Walking into the cell with a bowl of something a condemned man has asked for, being able to look him in the eye and know that I'd made an effort to arrange it for him, that always made the time we had left easier. When someone does their best, that creates an opening for a real connection. It made them talk about what they'd done and how they felt. Sometimes I feel... I don't know, a little disappointed, I guess, that some of my best deeds will never be known because everyone I've made an effort for took that to the grave with them. But then I remind myself that I didn't do it for my sake. None of this is about me. I want it to be in God's honor."

Tell me about a time when you thought, "I did a good job today. Shame no one will ever know about it."

"There was a prisoner called Troy Farris who came to the death house in 1999. He was so mad. He thought his family had betrayed him, and he was angry with the system for executing him, angry with the authorities. He was plain angry, simple as that. For most of the day, he refused to let me in. But as time wore on, he started listening a little, and after a while, he said, 'I take it out on everybody else, but the person I'm really angry with is myself.'"

Troy Farris lowered his guard and said that he would very much like to be saved but that there was no way God could forgive what he had done.

That made the chaplain fire on all cylinders.

"I knew I had him. We started talking, and he asked whether I really thought God could forgive him. I replied that I didn't think so; I *knew* so."

The prisoner said he had never dared open himself up and put his faith into something bigger than him, and Jim replied rather bluntly, telling him he didn't have much time left if he wanted to give it a try.

Right then, Troy Farris said, "You're right," and broke down in tears.

"I reached in through the cell door, and we prayed

together. He let it all out. But he wasn't talking to me; he was talking to God. He said, 'I'm a terrible person. I have blood on my hands; I have blood in my heart. I'm evil, but I've heard that you love and can forgive me. I don't deserve it, but I'm begging you to forgive me.' He just kept on crying, floods of tears. And then he said a long, long prayer."

Once he finished, Jim prayed for him. He thanked God for being willing to reach out and forgive the man, and for giving him a pure heart.

"I rounded off by pleading with Him to bring peace to Troy Farris, and as I said that, I saw his face change. The anger was gone. There was a calmness to his eyes that I hadn't seen earlier. He even laughed, and it felt so good to see that."

The prisoner got up and said he was looking forward to the execution and that he knew there was a place in Heaven waiting for him.

"He was really excited about it, and then he said, 'Hey, I heard about this baptism thing. Is there any way I could get baptized?' I shook my head and said that, sadly, that wouldn't be possible. A formal baptism would have required us to leave the death house, and that wouldn't be allowed so late in the day."

Troy Farris asked Jim whether he could go to the warden and check whether there was anything he could do, and so Jim did just that. He explained that the prisoner had given himself over to God and that he had expressed a desire to be baptized. As expected, the warden said it was out of the question to fill the font in the chapel and transfer him out of the death house. Jim made his way back to Troy Farris's cell to break the news, but his mind drifted to an occasion when he had baptized an old woman in a care home in Crockett, Texas.

"She asked me if I would come over and talk to her about Jesus, and she opened herself up to Christ that evening. She was around eighty, and she said, 'I want to be baptized. Tonight.' I told her I wasn't sure how that would work, but she was a resourceful old woman."

She called some of her closest friends, and they all came over. Her daughter, too. Jim looked around, went into her bathroom, and decided the bathtub would have to do.

"I filled it as best I could and then told her to get in while I knelt on the floor beside it. When she sat up after the baptism was over, she said, 'Praise God.' It was a wonderful evening. As I walked back to break the news to Troy Ferris that day, I found myself thinking about that woman and how much the baptism had meant to her, even though it wasn't exactly by the book. The truth is that there are different ways to baptize a person. It isn't what we'd call a scriptural baptism unless they're fully submerged in water, but I went back and talked to him and said that if he was really serious, we could work something out."

Troy Farris was sure. He wanted to be baptized. Jim went and grabbed a few towels, and they spread them out on the floor of the cell. Troy Farris got onto his knees, folded his arms across his chest, and Jim poured water over his head, making sure to hit his forehead.

"As the water ran down his face, you could really see the Holy Spirit absolving him of sin. We both prayed after that, and he was blissful. He said, 'This is such a special day for me. I know it's the last day of my life, but in some ways, it's also the first.' I had my little communion set with me, and we took communion together. One of the guards actually joined us."

They came in and kept you company?

"They came in mid-way through the ceremony and ended up hanging around. It was a great evening, spiritually."

How was it when he died?

"Very peaceful."

Troy Farris's last words were addressed to the family of the man he had killed. He said, "I can only tell you that Clark did not die in vain. I don't mean to offend you by saying that, but what I mean by that is, through his death, he led this man to God."

Sounds like a good day's work.

"It was a good day's work."

What you've just told me warmed my heart a little. You're a good person, Jim.

. . .

"I don't see myself as a good person."

Why not?

"Because of the things I've done.... I'm a little like Paul the Apostle. The things I should do, I don't. And the things I shouldn't, I do. That's something I grapple with all the time. I have done throughout my life. Don't get me wrong, I don't see myself as a bad person, but I've never excelled in anything. I guess that's why you'd be justified in calling me a failure, not a good person."

Have you ever wanted to save any of the death row prisoners?

"Yes, several times. Excell White, for example, who was also executed in 1999. He was one of the inmates who really made an impression on me. He'd been in prison for almost twenty-five years—for murder—but Excell was different. He was older, he was white, and he was quiet. I think what impressed me most was the fact that he was wearing the same shoes on the day he died that he'd been wearing when he first entered prison. That's pretty unusual; you really don't see that too often. He was very calm, too. We had no problems with him at all."

. . .

What does it tell you when a man has had the same pair of shoes for twenty-five years?

"That he was tired. That he was done. He told me he was ready. He said, 'I been here a long time. Living like this for twenty-five years ain't easy.' I remember him wanting to smoke and being very polite—calm and soft-spoken. At the end, when his time came, he left the cell quietly without any fuss. He didn't hesitate, but he wasn't in a hurry, either. It was more like, 'Okay, let's just get this over and done with.' He lay back on the gurney, they strapped him down, and the warden said, 'Do you have any final words?' And Excell replied, 'No, Sir, there's nothing I want to say.' He paused for a moment, and then he said, 'Just send me home.' He died peacefully, and I've often wondered about that. How many of them really feel that way in the moment? The younger men are often furious, angry, and combative. They have a tendency to make themselves the victim. They don't see themselves as criminals; they don't see themselves as violent. They don't see themselves as perpetrators. As time passes, with all the appeals and debates around the death penalty, they start to think of themselves as victims."

Let's just go back to the shoes for a moment. What do those shoes tell you?

"The other prisoners were always trying to get new shoes— shoes were an important symbol to them. They got folks out in the real world to buy sneakers for them. But Excell didn't care about any of that; he made do with the same pair for twenty-five years.

"I didn't think he seemed like the mean, violent kind of person you usually meet on death row. He was more of a gentle, quiet soul—but don't get me wrong. He'd done some terrible things; I know that."

Robert Excell White was sentenced to death for the murders of three people following a robbery near McKinney. Just before dawn on May 10, 1974, the thirty-six-year-old pulled up outside the Hilltop Grocery Store with a machine gun. Inside, he found seventy-three-year-old Preston Broyles, the owner, and Gary Coker and Billy St. John, two eighteen-year-old boys who had driven over to the gas station to top up the oil in their van.

Not long after the boys arrived, White and his two buddies marched into the store. They forced their victims onto the floor, took six dollars from the cash register and sixty from their wallets, and then started arguing about who was going to kill them. In the end, White fired several rounds into each of the three with his .30 caliber gun.

The day before the Hilltop murders, White had been over in Waco, drinking with a friend who was sharpening a knife for him. White grabbed the knife, stabbed the man to death, and stole several weapons, including the gun he used at the gas station.

A few days later, Excell White handed himself in to the police and confessed to all four murders. He quickly became known as "Excell the Executioner" in the press.

"A man who admits his guilt and is ready to be put to death.... He was so open to me and the process. I really did think he was a nice guy. I could have grown very fond of him. So yes, I would have spared his life, given half a chance.

Karla Faye Tucker's, too. I would have spared her life. I knew she had done bad things, and I knew she was guilty, but I could easily have lived next door to Karla Faye. She was just that sort of person. Excell, too.

"I already told you about the guy who wanted to hear 'Blue Clear Sky' on the radio. He was funny. I liked him a lot. I would have spared him as well. There was also another prisoner, a man by the name of David Lee Herman. When he arrived to be executed, he was loud and bullish. Not angry, just loud. He laughed a lot, and he started cracking jokes about lawyers pretty much as soon as he arrived. All afternoon, there were so many jokes about lawyers. Like this: What do you call five hundred lawyers on the bottom of the ocean?"

What?

"A good start."

Funny.

"As he lay on the gurney and they put the IV line into his arm, he was still cracking jokes. I guess it was probably down to nerves, but he kept it up right until the end."

The execution took place one day after David Lee Herman attempted to end his own life with a razor blade. According to Jim, he didn't want to give the state of Texas the satisfaction of killing him.

"That happened a few times. One guy had been stock-piling pills, and he took them all in one go just a few days before his execution date."

The man in question survived his suicide attempt.

"They took him to the hospital in Galveston and pumped his stomach, which isn't much fun at all."

On the morning of the man's scheduled execution date, he was still in intensive care.

"I went to the office to get an update, and the regional director was there. He told me they were trying to organize a plane for him and asked if I wanted to tag along. I said I would be happy to, and he told me to head straight to the airport, that he would make sure the plane stayed grounded until I got there."

The airplane was already on the runway when Jim arrived.

"The airport here is tiny. In any case, I got onboard, and we set off to collect the prisoner."

It was a cold, rainy day with thick cloud cover.

"We landed in the middle of nowhere, and suddenly, I see all these headlights racing toward us. Dusk had just fallen, but I think there must have been eighteen vehicles in total—police cars, vans from the Texas Department of Criminal Justice, and an ambulance. They had the plane completely surrounded.

"The police officers got out of their cars first, with guns drawn, and the medics then wheeled the man out of the ambulance.

"I got to them just as they were lifting him out. He was in a wheelchair, and he was still hooked up to a drip. They pushed him over to the airplane steps, helped him to his feet, removed the IV line, and bandaged his arms, then cuffed him."

The prisoner slowly started to climb the steps. The plan had been to sit him right behind the pilot, but that idea didn't go down well at all.

"The pilot said that if the inmate started causing trouble, he would be right in the firing line. He refused to take off if we sat him there."

Ultimately, they put the man at the rear of the plane, with Jim sitting just in front of him.

"We took off, and the flight can't have taken much more than twenty minutes. The inmate and I chatted a little, and he told me he wasn't feeling too good. He said it had been stupid to try to kill himself and that the medics had pumped him full of activated charcoal, that it had made him really thirsty."

The prisoner then asked Jim whether they did that sort of thing—transported people by air—very often.

"I told him that I knew of only two other inmates who had been flown in and that Karla Faye was one of them. He thought that was pretty cool."

Once they landed, Jim asked whether he could travel in the same vehicle as the inmate, and the guards agreed.

"We got into the back of a patient transport vehicle. A guard and driver were up front, and everyone else followed in the other vehicles."

The prisoner was back in a wheelchair, cuffed to the seat, and Jim sat beside him.

"I told him we were almost there and that it was time for a serious chat, and then I asked where he was spiritually. He said he was okay on that front, that he knew he was going to die, and that he had faith. For some reason, I didn't feel entirely comfortable with his answer. It was like there was something gnawing away at me. We'd reached Walls by that point, and as the car pulled up, he stopped talking. I asked him a question, but he just shook his head, so I held my tongue. That evening, I got a glimpse of how the death row prisoners must have felt when they first arrived and were taken the same route. I was right there with him, keeping him company on his final journey."

It proved to be a transformative experience for Jim.

"It was as though I was living that moment with him, as though I could understand the uncertainty and even the experience of what it was like. Driving through the yard and seeing the lights was an odd feeling. None of the other inmates were out, and the yard was empty; it was so peaceful at that eerie time of day. There are usually so many people rushing about when the transport vehicle arrives, but as we pulled up, it was so quiet. We got him out, and I turned to Mr. Jenkins, the warden, to ask if I could have a few minutes with the inmate. I said I knew it was late and that it was time for him to die but that I wasn't comfortable with the process yet." Jenkins agreed.

Once they got into the death house, the man repeated that he was thirsty. Jim gave him some water, and the inmate quickly knocked back six or seven glasses. The two men started talking, and Jim asked him about his faith. The inmate said that he had welcomed Jesus into his life, and they were just about to pray together when the warden came in.

"He asked if he could interrupt, and I said yes because you don't say no to the warden. Jenkins got onto his knees and looked the prisoner straight in the eye. 'Let me ask you one thing: have you reached a point in your life where you have accepted the Lord Jesus Christ as your savior?' The man replied, 'Yes, sir, I have.' With that, the warden got up, brushed the knees of his pants, and said, 'Good, then we can get started.'"

Jim said a quick prayer with the man, and the three then made their way through to the execution chamber.

"As soon as we set foot in there, he said he felt sick. He turned his head, and projectile vomited the black charcoal right up the wall. It was everywhere, from floor to ceiling. My goodness, it smelled so bad."

The warden had seen most things during his time on the job, and he simply shrugged and ordered someone to clean it up.

"So, a couple of people came in and rinsed off the vomit and changed the sheet, which was stained black. And after that, they got on with the execution."

The prisoner didn't say any last words that day, but as the drugs began to take effect, he began vomiting again.

"With his last spluttering breath, he got black vomit all over his face. Everybody was grossed out, but no one fainted or anything like that. You could hear people in the witness room groaning, though. I felt so bad for him, and I felt bad for his relatives, but there was nothing I could do. Once it was all over, we got his face cleaned up and tried to make him look presentable."

The chaplain sighs.

"It's just... He'd tried so hard to take his own life. And he let me see the execution process from his point of view because he allowed me in. I remember him saying he was afraid during the drive from the airport, that he didn't want it to happen. I asked him what he meant, and he said he didn't want any of the fuss that went hand in hand with an execution. That he didn't want to lie there with people watching him die; he just wanted to do it himself, his own way. But he never got that chance. I felt so sorry for him because he was feeling so bad. And to throw up like that... I don't know; it was all just too sad. That experience showed me the grief and helplessness these criminals have to go through. It also showed me the power of the state. The way they drove up to us, with all those vehicles and their guns drawn, all because of some helpless guy in handcuffs, hooked up to a drip and wearing nothing but a hospital gown. It felt like an oxymoron. An ironic set of circumstances."

All those armed guards for a man who could barely move.

"...And who didn't even have any underpants on. He managed to expose himself to the warden as he lay back on the gurney. Still, it was a good experience that taught me a lot."

What is it like for you when an execution doesn't go to plan? When, for example, the prisoner starts throwing up black vomit?

"I feel like we've let them down. One of the worst executions I was ever present for involved a man who was a drug addict. His veins were badly scarred, and the needle boys couldn't get the IV line in. They tried eleven times before they finally managed it, and by that point, the guy was pretty worked up.

I think it would have been a relatively uneventful execution if they'd managed it right away, but that wasn't what happened. He was so angry, and I had to tell the warden to wait before allowing the witnesses in so I could try to calm him down. He really wasn't in a good way.

"When they eventually began to inject the lethal cocktail, they did so with a little too much force for the man's narrow veins, which were damaged from years of abuse.

"There was so much pressure that the IV line popped right out, and the drugs were just spraying out into the room.

"The warden paused the execution and quickly closed the curtains before ushering the witnesses out of the adjoining rooms.

"They took the man's family back to the department and showed the victim's relatives outside. What worried us most was that too much of the drugs might have gone to waste. They weren't sure he had gotten enough of the first substance, and they didn't have any to spare, but the medical staff told us to continue with what we had left. This was back when we used three drugs: sodium pentothal, pancuronium bromide, and potassium chloride. The first was meant to sedate him, the second to paralyze the diaphragm and lungs, and the third to stop his heart. The IV line had come out while they were injecting the sodium pentothal, but they thought they probably had enough left to continue and render him unconscious."

Sounds like a bit of a gamble?

. . .

"Well, they were going to paralyze his diaphragm at some point anyway, so it wouldn't make much difference either way. Even with a small amount, he'd still be sedated. In any case, it was one of the worst executions I ever witnessed. I felt so helpless, and I really did feel bad for the prisoner by that point. It was an awful evening. It felt as though everyone in there was unprofessional and couldn't do their job properly. If the system is there to kill people, then it has to be as humane as possible. But it wasn't that evening."

Chapter Fourteen

*You have to really get down and dig into
the darkest areas if you want to move forward.*

1999

As the new millennium approached, Jim got a phone call from Alabama.

"A bunch of folks wanted to come out here and observe one of our executions. It happened all the time; people from all over the world came to Huntsville in the late nineties to see how we did things at the Walls Unit."

Jim welcomed the group and took them through his tasks for the day. One of the men was the director of a correctional facility over in Alabama, and he asked a lot of questions.

"He turned to me and said, 'Hey, why don't you come

over for one of our executions? Our chaplain is real young and inexperienced; you might be able to help him and give him some guidance.' I told him it would be an honor."

One Wednesday evening not long later, Jim attended an execution in Huntsville. It was 9:00 p.m. by the time he got home, but he immediately grabbed his bags and jumped back into the car. He drove all night, arriving at the prison just north of Mobile, Alabama, around 9:00 the next morning.

"I'd been on my feet all day, attended the execution, and then driven all night. They'd booked me a motel room, so I went over there, took a shower, changed my clothes, and then got a few minutes' rest. After that, I headed over to the prison."

They did almost everything differently in Mobile. Executions in Alabama still took place at midnight, and the death row inmates were allowed visitors in the lead-up.

"I sat with the prisoner and his family from midday until 10:15 that evening. It was great to see them all come together like that."

At 10:15, the prisoner said a final goodbye to his loved ones. He was searched and cuffed, with a chain around his legs, and Jim and the chaplain then accompanied him down a long corridor.

"It must have been four hundred meters long, poker straight with doors to the different wings on both sides. As we came out, someone shouted, 'Dead man walking!' It was so quiet you could have heard a pin drop. The only sound was his chain trailing on the floor."

They walked right to the far end in silence, and as the door opened, Jim heard a prisoner say, "We're with you, brother." That was all.

"We made our way into the death house, and the guards

opened a door, pointed to a cell, and told us to go inside. The man, the young chaplain, and I were all in the same cell. That would never have happened in Texas. There were always bars between the inmates and us there."

As they were making small talk, two guards came in. They had a disposable razor and a bowl of water, and they shaved a strip down the middle of his head while we kept chatting.

"He just sat there and let them do it. The whole thing was very relaxed."

They then pushed his pants up and shaved his left leg.

"They do that so the hair won't burn once the electricity starts flowing. They put a damp sponge on the inmate's head, too. It's just like in *The Green Mile* if you've ever seen that movie."

Once the guards were done, they left the prisoner with Jim and the young chaplain, and the three men continued to talk and pray.

"He was remorseful about what he had done, not at all aggressive or angry. And then the guards came back and took us through to the death chamber."

Waiting for them there was Alabama's version of Old Sparky: the electric chair known as Yellow Mama.

"I found it amazing and wonderful that every member of staff involved in the execution came in to shake his hand and say a few words. Bizarre, obviously, but very nice and respectful. They said their goodbyes, and then they strapped him down, and we said one last prayer before we were ushered out."

Jim and the chaplain found themselves in the same room as the condemned man's family: his wife and a couple of others. The victim's relatives were also present but in a separate room.

"He was given the chance to say a few last words, which he declined, and then they executed him in the chair. I think that execution probably affected me more than any in Texas ever did. It was just so much more graphic. Death is death, but it seemed to go on forever. When they switched on the power, he started convulsing; you could see the knots going up and down his arms. He was shaking all over, but I remember his thumbs best. He shook so hard that both popped out of joint."

Once he had been declared dead, the guards escorted his family out of the room, leaving Jim and the chaplain behind. The two men then made their way back into the death chamber, and another guard arrived with a gurney.

"I don't want to be too gruesome about it, but you know when you roast a turkey and you go to lift it out of the tray? The legs and wings come right off if you're not careful. That was how it felt with him in the chair. His body was so hot, literally fried. Just touching him was enough to burn you. It all felt so much more tangible than looking at someone who has just calmly passed away."

Jim can still remember the smell, too.

"Like burnt flesh and hair. I've encountered that smell several times in my life—you know, with people who've burned to death in their cars or houses—but to actually see someone die like that, it has an effect on you. I can smell it right now. I can still see the knots moving up and down his arms, too. And his thumbs. I can see his wife, who just slumped toward me. I can't imagine what it must be like to see someone you love go through that."

. . .

207

How much more inhumane would you say the electric chair is compared to the method used in Texas?

"Instinctively, I'd say it's a whole lot more inhumane. But rationally, I know that when a person is executed using electricity, it only takes two or three seconds before they don't actually feel a thing. Their body might still be alive, but their brain is fried. There are no more feelings, no more pain. It's just the current. From a practical point of view, it's probably a quicker death than in Texas. I'd guess the inmate doesn't feel anymore, but for the relatives watching... it must be completely awful for them."

What about the victim's relatives? Since many of the relatives in Texas feel disappointed that the prisoner is given too easy a death, would this be more to their liking?

"Oh, definitely. The most common thing I heard at execution after execution in Texas was, 'He didn't even suffer.' They wanted it to look more painful. So, yes, I think it would definitely bring more satisfaction to those relatives. Goodness knows that man seemed to suffer."

Jim tells me he is grateful for the experience but wouldn't want to do it again.

"I was exhausted, for one thing. I'd been awake for forty-eight hours straight. By the time we'd gotten him out of the chair and I left the prison, it was long after midnight, but I had to be back there to discuss the execution at eight the next morning. The director wanted to talk to everyone involved. I probably only got about four and a half hours of sleep that night. Forty-eight hours awake, followed by four and a half hours' sleep. I was like a zombie."

And did you feel like you were able to help the young chaplain?

"I think I did, but he also helped me. They didn't carry out as many executions as us, but theirs were much more intense, partly because of what they had to see and partly because the inmate got to spend time with his family. Watching them say goodbye to their loved ones in a way we didn't permit in Texas was heartbreaking."

What impact did it have on you?

"If you can manage to keep everything at a remove, it's bearable. But once you allow it to get to you, that's when it really starts wearing you down. I had a harder time than usual processing the execution in Alabama because it all felt a lot more real to me. Once you've seen a body convulsing like that, it gives you a whole load of clear memories. Still, the guards treated him with dignity, and he treated them with respect. I'm sure some of their executions didn't quite go so smoothly, but the process doesn't just affect the condemned prisoner; it affects everyone. And everyone views the execution from a different perspective."

What do you mean?

"In Texas, the warden and I were the only people other than the prisoner in the death chamber, and being there is completely different from sitting in one of the witness rooms. We all have our roles to play, but I've never been able to imagine what it must be like to be the person who injects the lethal cocktail. I'm not blaming them, and I'm not judging them, but I could never do something like that. On the other hand, I had no real problem standing alongside a prisoner as they died. In the execution process, it's just amazing to see how fragile we are—while also being so resilient."

How does it feel to relive these moments?

"I've had a lot to process at night since you and I started talking."

He smiles.

"I think maybe I should get therapy for PTSD or something. I've tossed and turned, thinking and reliving lots of things. It surprised me to realize how real it all still feels. By talking about it, it's like I've torn open a bunch of old wounds."

Is that good or bad?

. . .

"I've always seen it as good because the more you talk about something, the better you can process it. That's what I'm always telling people in my sermons: you have to really get down and dig into the darkest areas if you want to move forward. If a person tries to repress things too often, they become desensitized, which isn't healthy. These conversations have stirred things up inside me."

In me, too. I lie awake in my motel room, listening to the noisy AC unit and thinking about forgiveness and acceptance.

"And what have you come up with?"

That there are limits. You talk about second chances. Fine. But what about tenth chances? Or twentieth? Thirtieth? Where do you draw the line?

I tell him that, for years, I was convinced I had the best father on earth.

Like the day I had a fever and woke to a bouquet of roses and Dad sitting by my side, having driven all night to get home and see how I was. I've never felt as loved as I did in that moment, and a bouquet of flowers has never been more beautiful.

When he looked at me, he did it in a way no one else could. And when he laughed, there was nothing funnier than to laugh along.

Those gray eyes could be full of such love, but a moment

later, they could be filled with hate. I spent my life trying to work out how to act in order to keep the nice version of him around—the one who loved me more than anything else. How to keep the monster away.

"So what broke you in the end?" Jim asks.

We'd been to a birthday party at Dad's place, and he'd had one of his outbursts. My older brother and I had both been kicked out, which wasn't unusual, but what was different was that I had a new boyfriend with me, and he was shocked. He asked me and my brother how often that sort of thing happened and what would happen later. We told him there was usually a few weeks of silence, and then we'd call Dad, and everything would go back to normal.
   "You call him?" he asked. "Why do you call him?"
   My brother and I looked at each other, and it was as though we suddenly didn't have any answers. We decided enough was enough—that we wouldn't call this time.

I smile at Jim, and I feel proud.
   He waits for me to go on.

That was almost fifteen years ago, but we still haven't called. For me, it's over. Every family party I go to now, every Christmas I celebrate... I can do it without a lump in the pit of my stomach, without having to worry about him exploding. I don't think anyone who hasn't experienced that sort of conflict can really appreciate the silence once the war is finally over.

"I'm glad you're doing better now, but it still affects you. You don't need to be in touch with your father in order to forgive him."

People always say that the older you get, the more you understand your parents, but the opposite is true for me. I understand my father less and less the older I am. When I was pregnant, sometime around seven months, I did a report on homeless people and found myself face-to-face with a man brandishing a knife. God, in that moment, my first instinct was to turn my head 180 degrees to look for something to hit him with, and all to protect my unborn child. I spent a long time thinking about that later—how desperately I wanted to protect my baby and how willing my father was to hurt his own children. I just can't make sense of it. Since you and I started talking, I've felt the urge to ask him, but I know I wouldn't get any sensible answers.

"Are you sure? He might have changed over time, too."

Maybe, but let's change the subject. A question of practicalities, apropos the different times executions were carried out in Alabama and Texas. Why was it moved from midnight to 6:00 p.m.?

· · ·

"Because of the courts, the appeals process. The people working on the executions also had their regular jobs to do. They had to be at work at eight in the morning, and then they worked until the execution was over and were back again at eight the next day. That meant a lot of long, tough days. It ground people down, and it was hard on the families —both the prisoner's and the victim's—to have to sit around waiting until midnight. And then there are the state courts, the Supreme Court, and the federal district courts. If they've got an appeal underway, all those people have to stay at the office, too."

Despite all that, Jim says he was grateful for the executions he attended that took place at midnight.

"It gave me more meaningful time to work with the prisoners. These days, the inmates are taken to the death house to meet the chaplain at 2:30 in the afternoon, and four hours later, they're dead."

It's not so easy to give them a ticket to Heaven under those circumstances, I guess.

"Exactly. And that's all anyone wants when they die... a ticket to Heaven."

Chapter Fifteen

Whenever our leaders kill in the name of justice, we are all diminished.

2000

On March 16, 2000, Jim Brazzil was asked a question that had never come up before.

Timothy Lane Gribble had been sentenced to death for the rape and murder of Elizabeth Jones, a thirty-six-year-old woman who worked as a manager on the NASA shuttle project, and he asked the chaplain if he would read his last words for him.

"He'd been in prison a long time, and he had admitted his guilt. He really was very remorseful."

Gribble had gone over to Elizabeth Jones's house as a

roofer. He left her property at the end of the working day, but just two hours later, he returned, claiming to have left his wallet there. Jones let him in, and when she failed to show up for work the next day, her colleagues called the police, who quickly identified Gribble as a person of interest. He denied all involvement in his first few interviews, but once he was eventually arrested, he confessed and led the police to her body in a remote area of woodland.

"Gribble came to the death house full of regret. We shared a spiritual experience there. He wrote a letter to the victim's relatives, explaining what he felt, and asked if I would read it out as part of his last words."

Jim spoke to the warden, who checked the letter and gave him the green light.

"In the death chamber that day, Gribble began to speak, but after a moment or two, he said, 'Chaplain Brazzil will read the rest of my statement,' and then he handed me the sheet of paper."

To the Jones Family: Please accept my sincerest apology and regrets for what happened to your loved one. It was truly a horrible thing that I did, and I regret it deeply. I do not know if this will ease your pain, but I truly pray that this will help you find peace. I am sincerely truly sorry.

For the Weis Family: The same is true. I regret what happened.

(...)

The death penalty is an unnecessary punishment for society who has other means to protect itself. You cannot rectify death with another death. Whenever the state chooses to take a life and take the power of God into their own hands, whenever our leaders kill in the name of justice, we are all diminished.

(...)

Just know that I go with God.

"Gribble himself then said: 'I just want to pray a chant; do what you have to do.'"

He chanted?

"Yes, he prayed and chanted right until the very end."

How did it feel to read his statement?

"It was tough. I was nervous."

The first part you read was fairly standard, but the second part is pretty political.

"Very political. But those were his words."

Sure, but he got you to say them.

.   .   .

"Mmhmm. Even now, I have a hard time being political. As a chaplain, my job isn't necessarily to make judgments on things. I'm there to offer compassion and love. I'm there to facilitate forgiveness or do whatever it takes for the person to make amends with God."

When you talk about forgiveness, I always feel a little uneasy. I don't want to forgive everything; I really don't.

"Yes, I can understand that. But for me, forgiveness has played a part in some of the moments that had the biggest impact on me. That's when real change happens. You can't experience freedom if you won't forgive."

What would it do for me if, for example, I forgave my father?

"You wouldn't be angry anymore. That intense feeling of hate would disappear. You won't ever like him, and I'm not saying you should hug and make up; it's more about letting go of your anger and opening your heart so you can give that part of it to your husband and son instead, for example."

Or myself.

"Or yourself. Right now, these feelings are taking up space in your heart—in a negative sense—but you could use that space for something positive instead. It wouldn't be for his sake if you forgave him, but your own. I saw that so clearly whenever I took part in mediations. Once someone has expelled the poison from their own body, all the hate and anger, they're able to transform it into forgiveness... that liberates a person."

Jim remembers one case in particular.

"This kid was eighteen or nineteen when he committed his crime. He had a step-sister, and though this girl was a good few years younger than him, they started a physical relationship. He got another boy involved, and she didn't know how to say no to him, so before long, the three were all in a relationship together. It was too much for the girl, and one day, she told him that she couldn't do it anymore and that she needed to tell her mom. That terrified the boy, and he strangled her. He then called his buddy, and they dumped her body in a culvert.

"The girl's mother came home, and the young man said he didn't know where she was. He spent the next week helping to put up missing person flyers for her.

"They searched and searched, but I think it was ten days before they finally found her body. The boy was tried and sentenced, and his stepmother chose to go through mediation with him. She wanted to confront him because he had been such a source of support for her during her daughter's disappearance. She felt anger and hatred, not just over her daughter's death but because he had misled her, lied to her, and helped her put up posters when all the while he was responsible for killing her girl. She was so angry about that."

Jim tells me that the woman started drinking to numb the grief and depression that hit her. She lost her job as a result, and in an attempt to get her life back on track, she began going to therapy, which involved straightening things out with the people around her. That was the reason she decided she wanted to see her step-son.

"We started the dialogue process, and... my goodness, he really opened up to me during our preparatory conversations."

Before long, the time came for the meeting itself. The woman had thrown up right before she arrived, and two nights earlier, she had also fallen off the wagon. Going through the mediation process was incredibly hard for her, and she was nervous, nauseous, and angry. Jim reassured her as best he could, and when he went out into the corridor to get the inmate, he found him throwing up into a trash can.

"He said it was the worst thing he had ever been through, and I told him I was in control of the situation. He said that was good because he wasn't, and then he broke down in tears. I told him he would be just fine and that all he had to do was sit there and listen and let her talk. Hold off on answering."

They made their way into the room together, and Jim asked the guard to hang back in case anything went wrong.

The minute the session got underway, the woman started shouting at her stepson.

"She really raised her voice, saying that he had tricked her, that he had taken her daughter from her and pulled the wool over her eyes. She really let loose on him."

When relatives start shouting like that, do you ever tell them to stop, or do you just leave them to it?

. . .

"It depends if they get up or not. If they do, I stop them. But if they stay in their seat, I just let them say what they need to say."

The man sat quietly, watching the woman as she spoke. Once she was done, it was his turn.

"He opened his mouth and said that she was right. He said that he deserved whatever she wanted to do to him because he had betrayed her in all the ways it was possible to betray a person."

The woman started crying when the man said he didn't deserve anything good.

"She hadn't realized how she would react to him simply laying himself bare and admitting to everything."

The woman had brought a photo album with her, and she put it down in front of him.

"She had so many pictures of him from his childhood—pictures of the two kids together."

They started flicking through the album. Hesitantly at first, then with a comment here or a memory there. Laughter.

"For him, sitting there and re-living all that... and for her, seeing the little boy he had once been, who had lived in her home... Once they began to reconnect with each other, her expression changed completely. Her outbursts became much milder, too. And a look of calm spread across his face. They both changed in a really fantastic way.

"The young man reached a point where he could give her a wholehearted, sincere apology, and she could reply with an honest 'I forgive you' in return. That made a world of difference to them both."

They flicked right through the photo album together, laughing and chatting about how precious it was and how beautiful the woman's daughter had been.

"When she got up, she asked me whether she was allowed to hug him. Protocol says no, but I told her that, of course, she could. And so she walked around the table and gave him a big hug."

She said she missed him even though he had taken so much from her. He replied that he knew it wouldn't make any difference how much he said he was sorry.

"The meeting ended with the woman thanking him for agreeing to see her. She said it had given her her life back. I thought those were such powerful words. She left that room a different woman from the one she had been when she arrived. Seeing the power of forgiveness, the way God transformed these people... it was wonderful."

Jim smiles at the memory.

"I was actually involved in another similar situation with a man who robbed a convenience store over in Abilene. He raped and murdered the teenage girl who worked there, a real brutal story."

The girl's mother requested a mediation meeting. Until that point, the prisoner had chosen to keep a lot of things to himself.

"He claimed to be a gang member, a tough guy, and so they put him in ad. seg., or administrative segregation. An isolation cell, in other words. He had no contact with any of the other prisoners, which was his own choice."

As they got ready for the session, the mother came in with much the same attitude as the previous woman Jim told me about. They sat down, and she told the prisoner that he deserved to be locked up. He replied, "Yes, ma'am, I do." The woman then said that she needed him to answer one question. She wanted to know whether her daughter had suffered prior to death.

The man sat quietly for some time, and then he broke down in tears.

"He said that he wished he could remember but that he had been high and drunk and that much of his memory was gone. He said he remembered being on top of her, having sex with her, but that he didn't remember actually killing her. He said he wished he could tell the mother she didn't suffer, but he was pretty sure that wasn't true. It was hard for her to hear that. He was so honest with her about everything."

They took a break, and Jim escorted the prisoner out of the room. He was overwhelmed by the situation, and he told Jim that his body was crying out for the woman's forgiveness. That, if it helped, he would gladly lie down on the table and let her gut him because she deserved the peace of mind.

"Forgiveness is a powerful thing. The fact that a hardened old criminal like that could be transformed by a grieving mother coming in and being willing to forgive him is proof of that."

And was she? Willing to forgive him?

"Yes. She said that the only reasons she had come were to get an answer to her question and to say that she forgave him—eye to eye."

The prisoner found that very hard to believe.

"He was completely taken aback and said, 'You're willing to forgive me?' She told him she already had, and he broke down in tears. And then he said that maybe he would forgive himself one day, too. It was so powerful, being able to see how mercy and forgiveness can cause hatred and pain—

things a person has felt for years—to melt away in just a few short hours."

I've noticed that you almost always say, "They had sex with them," rather than, "They raped them." Is that your choice of words or theirs?

"Both, I guess. Rape involves so many things I can't stand."

Well, yes, it's not a pleasant thing.

"I think it's the act itself I really struggle with—forcing another person to have sex with you. I just can't make sense of it. To me, making love to my wife is so holy."

But that's exactly my point. Sex and rape aren't the same thing, so why say it was one when it was the other?

"You're right. I have a few stories where it was nothing but rape. And I have another experience from a mediation meeting with a lady who'd been raped. The man pretended to be a real estate agent and lured her into a building where she wanted to rent an apartment. He raped her. He forced her onto her knees and made her perform oral sex on him before he penetrated her. She later managed to identify him, and he was sentenced to twenty years in prison. The mediation session was her idea, but once we were all there, she only said one thing, 'You know, I'm not out to hurt you, but there's something I want to say. When you put that thing in my mouth, and you forced me to suck on it, all I could think was, my God, he's got a tiny dick.'"

Jim laughs.

"You should have seen his face. Saying those words allowed her to take back control. It gave her the upper hand and broke his power over her. I thought she was so brave to be able to say something like that to him."

Off the top of your head, how many mediation meetings would you say you have taken part in?

"I probably did thirty or forty, mostly for rape. Some for murder."

So roughly fifteen to twenty rape survivors wanted to meet their rapists?

"Yes. The request for mediation has to come from the injured party. They have to be a close relative of the victim if the victim is dead or the victim themselves. And I have to say that every single one of them was a stronger person afterward."

Jim says he has never experienced a bad mediation session. The injured party had to go through months and months of preparation, filling in all kinds of paperwork and reliving the event with him several times, all with the aim of working out their anger and starting to process it. Jim would then make an assessment of the application and share his thoughts with the board, who would go through the case and determine whether he had come to the right conclusion.

So, first, you decide whether the injured party is suitable, and then, you decide on the prisoner.

"Yes, they have to meet certain criteria."

The convict had to confess to their crime. He—and it is almost always a he—must also have been in prison for at least two years prior to the start of the mediation process. If both parties were willing to continue after the initial preparatory conversations, Jim would visit the inmate and give him various documents to fill in. After that, he met with the victim and told them he had spoken to the prisoner, and they were cooperative. There would then be a period of back and forth between the two, with yet more conversations and paperwork.

"It takes several months to plan, conversation after conversation in which we really dig down into what happened and the things they need to work through. Once I feel like they're ready, when I believe the victim is strong enough, I'll decide that it's time. I'm often pretty straight to the point as we're going through the process. You have to get them to talk about it, to tell you what happened. And in the end, I think they both grow stronger from being able to share that."

· · ·

You're saying that both the rapists and their victims get stronger?

"That's correct."

You've conducted some thirty to forty mediation sessions over the years. How many would you say haven't taken place?

"The majority, particularly on death row. What makes it tricky there is that the inmate has to have confessed to their crime for mediation to take place, but almost everyone on death row keeps appealing against their sentence until the very end. By confessing, they're essentially signing their own death warrant."

Could you tell me a little about the rape victims who wanted to meet these men?

"Most of them were white women between twenty-five and thirty-five years of age. They'd often put on a few pounds— sometimes more than a few—after the rape; they didn't take good care of themselves, and they'd become emotionally unstable. They were victims in the real sense of the word. I followed up with many of them, and seeing their transformation after the meeting was remarkable."

Jim's thoughts turn to one woman in particular.

"She went to the grocery store one day, completely unaware that a man had been watching her. When she got back to her car with her bags, he shoved her in and locked the door. He gripped her throat and tried to pull her panties down. She had the presence of mind to tell him to stop, that she'd let him do whatever he wanted if he would just stop choking her."

The man was so taken aback that he stopped.

"He let her compose herself, and then he continued— just shoved it in and started having sex with her. Raped her, or whatever you want to call it."

It was rape, Jim.

"It certainly was. He reached up and grabbed her throat again, but she pushed his hands away and said, 'I told you; you're not allowed to hurt me.' That unsettled him so much that he pulled out and ran off. He didn't finish."

The woman called the police, but they failed to make an arrest.

Later that evening, however, the same man waited for another woman as she left her home to get the mail. He attacked her, raped her, and choked her to death. The similarities between the two incidents quickly led the police to connect her death to the earlier rape. The man had left DNA evidence in the dead woman's body, and they managed to track him down and arrest him. He was sentenced to death for her murder, but the police never brought any charges for the first rape.

"Her case was never solved, but we held a mediation session all the same, and with his confession, she went from being a victim to a survivor to a warrior."

Are those the different steps, in your view? Victim, survivor, and warrior?

"In my opinion, yes. I've seen those phases in many different people."

I think I have a good life today, but I still don't want to forgive my father. I don't want to absolve him of guilt.

"I can tell. I'd say you're stuck somewhere between being a victim and a survivor."

I understand why you would say that, but it still upsets me a little.

"I don't mean to upset you; it's just an observation. When a person has been hurt by someone, it's like having a rubber band holding you back. You try to walk away, but because of all the bitterness and hate in your body, you always end up going back and having it hurt you all over again. You want to leave, but you're constantly being pulled back."

. . .

So, what's the solution?

"You have to turn to face that rubber band and start pulling on it, working at it until it slackens. And once you've stretched it out far enough, it can't hurt you quite so much."

And how does someone go from being a victim to a survivor to a warrior? What are the steps?

"When you're a victim, everything in your life carries you back to the pain, in my experience. It takes you back to the perpetrator—the pain you feel, the anger you feel, the evil. It's always there; it permeates your life. You try to leave it behind, but as long as that anger is still there, it'll drag you back to whatever happened."

Jim has seen it countless times in the victims' families' lives after their loved ones were murdered. They try to move on, but just like that, a new trial is scheduled, or new information comes to light.

"And that emotional rollercoaster constantly drags them back to the perpetrator. 'What would I do if I saw him?' or 'What would I do if he turned up at my home?' They become extremely watchful and hyper-vigilant, always looking over their shoulders. Their entire world is turned upside down. But once they finally understand that this person can't hurt them anymore and that the worst has already happened, they reach a stage that is easier to control.

They start finding the courage to go out, one step at a time, moving out of their comfort zone. I've seen people who literally lock themselves in their homes with the windows closed and the curtains drawn—people who wouldn't answer the phone or turn on the TV. They shut the world out because that felt comforting to them. But, little by little, they started making an effort, like going out onto the porch or the sidewalk, onto the street. It might be just a few meters from the house, but that was a big victory for them. And with that, they managed to move on."

And is that when a person becomes a survivor?

"That's when they become a survivor. Surviving is just as closely bound to the event as being a victim is—because what exactly are you surviving? You're surviving the loss, the crime, whatever the person in question did to you. And even if you do manage to set foot outside, your entire life is still closely linked to the crime. But a person gets sick of that after a while. Sick of the tiredness, sick of the crime, sick of the depression, and sick of the self-pity. Then, a person reaches a point where they don't want things to be like that anymore, and they start to do something about it. Rather than being a survivor, they become a so-called proactivist. They're in a place where they can re-enter life and make a strategy for how to get over it and defeat it. That's where the warrior comes in."

What is a warrior like?

. . .

"A warrior has made an active decision to move on from what happened, to free themselves from their own chains. They've dug deep into the darkest corners, looked their pain straight in the eye, worked with it, and found the key to moving on. It's a little like what we touched upon earlier when we were talking about guilt. The victim becomes a warrior when they can grab the event by the horns and take control of it. It takes a lot for a person to accept the event and make it a part of who they are. The person must accept that they will never go back to the person they were, but that this new version of them can be a warrior."

I want to be a warrior.

"In my experience, it comes after forgiveness. How a person handles guilt, anger, and forgiveness is the key to living a healthy life. Forgiving isn't the same as saying something is okay. It simply means that it can't hurt you any longer. With forgiveness, you loosen the grip a person has over you and the past."

I don't think I'm ready for that.

"That's why I said you're caught somewhere between victim and survivor. Forgiveness isn't easy; it has to come from the very depths of your heart, where the wound hurts most. And it isn't just about making a concrete, active decision. It needs to be reinforced again and again. But, with time and patience, I think it will come. Even for you."

What impact did the mediation sessions have on the inmates?

"We often had to put them under close watch—security watch, rather than suicide watch. They weren't expected to work or do anything else the day after the session. Since the process was so painful, they were often completely drained, and sometimes that made them physically sick. None of them—not one—ever said they regretted going through with it, though. I think the mediation program is the best thing about the corrections system in Texas. It should be used much more widely."

I was just thinking about suicide in prison. You mentioned a few attempts you encountered. That must be a tough part of the job.

"It is. I was on my way to meet an inmate who had asked for a few things once, and as I passed another of the cells, I saw a man hanging there. He had tied a rope from the top bunk. I called for help, and we got him down, but he started crying, asking why we'd gone to the effort of saving him when all he wanted was to die. I spent a while talking to him, and he seemed okay. But four days later, he successfully managed to take his own life."

Jim shakes his head.

"A lot of men who die by suicide in prison don't really mean to kill themselves. They just want someone to pay attention to them. Those are the saddest cases."

What's the final straw for them?

"The hopelessness. They have no future, no tomorrow. They can't live with their memories. Many of the inmates on death row feel that way. I once met a guy who was a serial killer, and he said to me, 'You don't know what it's like to wake up every morning with all these people's faces on your mind.' Michael Lockhart was his name."

Michael Lockhart had been sentenced to death in three American states: Florida, Indiana, and Texas.

"His was a really interesting execution. He was the only person I ever met who had been sentenced to death in multiple states. Sitting across from me, he didn't try to apologize or justify himself. He just told me what he had done and said that the day he was arrested was the best day of his life because he knew he would never hurt another woman."

Jim tells me that Michael Lockhart explained that his big sister had abused him from the age of thirteen. He was convicted of the rape and murder of a sixteen-year-old girl in Griffith, Indiana; the rape and murder of a fourteen-year-old girl in Florida; and the murder of a police officer who tried to arrest him in Beaumont, Texas.

"He claimed that the girls he killed looked like his sister. And then he said he wanted to make one last call to his daughter, whom he hadn't spoken to in years. I arranged that for him, and they both cried. He said that he wanted her to know he was guilty, that he did everything he was accused of, and that she shouldn't be angry with the system. He told her he deserved to die but that he didn't want to go before he got the chance to tell her to make the most of her life, that he was sorry he had let her down, and that he wished her well. It was a powerful conversation."

Chapter Sixteen

I can honestly say that, on execution day, the majority of the victims' relatives are still right where they were when their loved one died. No one has helped them to process their feelings.

2000

Two years after Jim and Janice's divorce, Janice remarried.

"They are still married to this day. I hope she's happy. We meet up from time to time when the kids are involved. They actually invited us to Thanksgiving one year, but it felt pretty awkward."

Around this time, Jim also decided he wanted to get married again, but Bobbie had different ideas.

"She was scared. She already had three ex-husbands,

and she didn't want a fourth. I proposed to her over and over again, but she just kept saying no. It became a matter of conscience for me. I wanted to be with her, but I also felt like I was compromising my faith."

The early millennium brought another new challenge for Jim: the first woman to be executed following the media circus that had arisen around Karla Faye Tucker's death.

"With Betty Beets, everything was different. Betty was a lot older than Karla Faye. You looked at her, and she was so worn out and... what's the word? She was hardened, I guess. Hardened from a tough life."

Betty Lou Beets was put to death on February 24, 2000, for the murder of her fifth husband, Jimmy Don Beets. She shot and buried him in the backyard, and when the police dug up the garden to look for him, they also found the body of her fourth husband. He, too, had been shot with a pistol of the same caliber, and yet Betty Beets was never charged over his death.

"I remember that they brought her over the night before the execution, and I went to the death house to talk with her. She said, 'It's not right what they're doing. They're not taking all the circumstances into account.' She was open with me about killing the two men, but she also said that both had beaten her black and blue."

Jim tells me that during one of their conversations, she asked whether he thought she looked like someone who could have killed such a big man, dragged his body down the stairs and out into the yard, dug a grave, and buried him there.

"Betty was a small woman, and as I sat there looking at

her, she answered her own question. She said, 'No, I couldn't have done it on my own. I had plenty of help.'"

According to Jim, she hinted that her family had been involved, but she never came out and said it.

"I found her so sad. You couldn't feel God's joy and presence in her company. It was all Betty's sadness and suffering."

Did you believe she would get to Heaven?

"Yes, I did. We spoke about it quite a bit. She wasn't filled with joy and purpose like Karla Faye, but she felt that He was her savior and would bring her peace and strength."

You've come into contact with all sorts of minorities in prison: women, Latinos, and Black prisoners. Is there, in your opinion, any difference in terms of ethnicity on death row? In terms of the sentences handed down?

"No."

No?

"No."

· · ·

I've got the statistics here. The odds of a white man in the U.S. ending up in prison is one in 106. For a Latino, the figure is one in thirty-six. But for a Black man, the likelihood of ending up behind bars is one in fifteen.

"Okay."

In the free world, just over thirty percent of people in this country are either Black or Latino. But when you step inside the prison walls, those figures change dramatically, rising to well over fifty percent of the prison population. Do minorities really commit that many more crimes?

"Yes. I don't know how else to explain it. I'm not an expert, and it's honestly not something I ever give much thought to, but I do know that as far as their education and opportunities are concerned, they might not have gotten the right chances in the free world. I don't know. I've never had the sense that anyone thinks, 'Oh, he's Black, so let's frame him.'"

When I wrote my book about the death penalty, I looked at the statistics of everyone who had been sentenced to death during the past five years. Sixty percent of them were Black, despite the fact that only fifteen percent of the broader population in the free world is Black. To me, those figures say that Black people are being targeted.

· · ·

"You have to understand the culture they live in and the lifestyle they have. When I was a young man, I lived in Temple—which was actually a pretty racist place, now that I think about it. They all were back then. As a matter of fact, there's a town not far from here called Jasper. I had a friend from there, and I visited him there once. There was a gas station there, and it had a sign saying, 'If you're black, don't let the sun go down on you in Jasper.'"

Jim tells me it was much the same in his hometown. There were restrooms for colored people and restrooms for whites; drinking fountains for colored people and drinking fountains for whites. One of the stores there had an escalator alongside a set of regular steps, and the sign above the escalator read: "Whites only."

"It was a place divided by skin color. There was the Black side of town and the white side of town, and the majority of houses on the white side were pretty much okay. Temple wasn't a rich place. I lived in the poorer area, of course, but that was still nothing compared to the hovels the Black folks lived in."

What does that have to do with crime?

"I'm being honest with you here, and I'm not sure whether I should say this or not, but for a while, I had a job repairing AC units, which meant I also visited some of the Black homes. They were filthy, real hovels, but they had brand new cars outside—fancy Cadillacs and Lincolns. The Black folks put more money into making other people think they had money than into their homes or kids. I saw it with my own eyes, though, of course, that was just in one small town; I can't say how things were across the country."

But that has more to do with the image a person wants to give the outside world than proof of crime. To me, from a purely statistical point of view, it just doesn't add up that fifteen percent of the population can be responsible for so much more crime—to the extent that sixty percent of people on death row are Black. The figures tell me that the system is statistically unfair and biased. To me, they show systemic racism. Don't you see that?

"No, I don't, probably because I grew up here. I saw the kind of crime being committed in Temple, and I know who was responsible."

So why do you think Black people commit more crimes than white?

"Because the Black people my age, they had tough lives. They were segregated and were treated as second-class citizens, and as they grew older, they acted that way. There was a lack of education because most of them dropped out of school. They couldn't read or write. I can't tell you how many times I gave someone a bill after working at their house, and they couldn't read it. I had to read it for them. They were uneducated. That might be because they weren't

241

given the opportunity, but they were uneducated all the same."

But the statistics we're talking about relate to the present day. They're not from back when you were young. It's still the case that a Black person is five times more likely to end up in prison than a white person.

"Okay. Well, I don't have any answers to that; I really don't. Maybe it's just my prejudice talking, as a white person, but I think people play the race card far too often, and rather than focusing on the crimes, they focus on skin color. I've never really given much thought to it. I just worked with the people who were there to work with."

So, do you think today's figures seem logical because Black people still commit more crimes?

"Yes."

And why do they still commit more crimes, in your opinion?

"Because of the places they live and because their gangs are much more violent. To me, gang criminality is one of the most frightening parts of modern America. There are white gangs, too, and Hispanic. The Hispanic gangs are probably the most dangerous of them all."

It's the fastest-growing, for sure.

"The fastest-growing and most dangerous. The majority operate on a blood-in, blood-out basis. Bloodshed is the only way to join the gang, and the only way you can leave is if they shed *your* blood. It's so brutal. Illegal immigrants are arriving in the United States all the time, and they end up staying and flying beneath the radar. These kids don't stand a chance of getting an education or making something of themselves, so they take from those who do. Because of the minority issues, that's what the Black folks do, too. They don't think they have any other option, and even if they do, they don't make the most of it. But I can see that things are changing. I have some wonderful friends who are Black, and I have some wonderful friends who are Hispanic. I don't consider myself to be a racist, even though I grew up in a racist environment."

Let's get back to the year 2000.

"That was when I made the biggest mistake of my career."

One confession would eventually go on to change the course

of Jim Brazzil's career. It was made by a man named Rickey McGinn on September 27, 2000.

"He lived in a place called Brownwood, and his wife was a professional ten-pin bowler. Her job took her all over the country, so she often left her twelve-year-old daughter with him. At the time of the incident in question, she was in Fort Worth, and he was back home with the girl. He raped her, killed her with an axe, and then hid her body."

When Rickey McGinn reported his stepdaughter missing to the authorities, he told detectives that he and the girl had gone fishing, that they had a few beers, and that she then walked off. Her body was found in a culvert three days later.

Circumstantial evidence led to McGinn being convicted of her murder. Traces of blood found in his car and on the axe proved to be a match for the girl, but he continued to protest his innocence, claiming that the real killer was still out there somewhere.

"He'd come close to being executed once before, but he was given a stay because he requested DNA testing, which was pretty new at the time. He said, 'If you do a DNA test, you'll see I'm innocent.' So, they did, and it was a perfect match. Rather than clearing him, it was the final nail in the coffin."

Rickey McGinn's was one of the more high-profile executions Jim was involved in, and there were countless TV cameras and news teams outside the Walls Unit that day.

"He claimed the court was rigged and told everyone who would listen... the warden and the world. No one believed him. His mother was an elderly woman involved in the

Pentecostal church. She had no teeth, and she got around with a walker. My goodness, I can still hear her saying, 'Oh, my precious baby.' She spoke to the press that day, and everything she said had to do with the fact that the authorities were about to kill her beloved, innocent son."

Just before the execution was scheduled to take place, McGinn asked to talk to the chaplain one last time.

"He came to me and said he had done what he was accused of. He was crying. We walked through to the chamber together, and he hopped up onto the gurney. He didn't struggle, didn't put up any resistance whatsoever. He just hopped up there and laid down. The team fastened the restraints and inserted the IV line pretty quickly. They then left the room, and he and I were alone together. I asked if he wanted to pray, and he said yes. So we prayed."

As they did, the witnesses came in. By that point in time, the rules had changed to allow relatives of both the victim and the condemned prisoner to be present for the execution in two separate rooms. The victim's family came in first.

"The murdered girl's mother was the first to arrive, and she was in floods of tears. That wasn't so uncommon among the victims' relatives. Being there forced them to relive the loss of the person they had loved so much, and they found being in prison frightening. It was very emotional to be so close to their loved one's killer, too. She walked right up to the window, tipped her head toward the glass, and looked straight down at McGinn's face. He didn't meet her eye, but I saw a couple of tears. She just kept crying, but he never looked up at her.

"After that, they opened the door to the other witness room, and I told him that his mom was on her way in. She pushed her walker right up to the window and did the same thing: she tipped her head toward the glass and cried. I can still picture her so clearly; the tears flooded her cheeks. 'Oh, my precious baby.' That was all she said that afternoon. 'My precious baby.'"

Once everyone was in place, the warden asked Rickey McGinn if he had any last words.

McGinn said, "Tell everybody I said hi, that I love them, and I will see them on the other side, okay? And now, I just pray that if there is anything against me that God takes it home. I don't want nobody to be mad at nobody. I don't want nobody to be bitter."

Jim has never forgotten the moment McGinn took his final breath. The prisoner had been crying, and Jim watched as a tear rolled down his cheek and caught on the very tip of a hair.

"I had a habit, after looking down at the prisoner and watching him die, of glancing over to see what was going on in the witness rooms. And that was when it struck me. I must have seen it before, but it had never really occurred to me."

As Jim turned toward the windows that day, he saw two mothers. One of them had lost her child eighteen years ago, but the other was losing her son right there and then. Their heads were only a thin wall apart, both leaning into the glass, and tears were running down their cheeks.

"That evening, I had a vision—more clearly than I ever had before. I thought that if I could just get a chance to reach out to these victims, I would be able to make a real difference in their lives. The woman, the victim's mother, had no church, no pastor; she had no one who really cared about her."

Just like that, Jim realized he had been helping the wrong people. The victims' relatives were often in real need of supportive conversations, and these simply weren't offered to them. He wanted to be able to give them a sense of hope they didn't currently have.

That's quite the turnaround. After being so sure of your calling for so long, I mean.

"Death took on a whole new meaning for me; loss took on new meaning for me. I could see it from the victim's side, those left behind. I wanted to help them find peace."

Once the thought had taken root, Jim couldn't shake it, so he contacted the head of Victim Services.

"I was in my office, and she came over to talk. I told her that I really felt for the victims. I knew how much work we put in with the inmates and their families at the prison, and I was frustrated the same effort wasn't made with those left behind, people who were also in desperate need of help. She said I was welcome to switch sides, to come over and do that with them."

Jim told her that Victim Services had certain guidelines he wouldn't be able to follow. For example, he needed to be able to talk to people about Jesus.

"And she said, 'You can talk about Jesus however much you want. You can pray. Anything you do with the prisoners, you can do with them.'"

Jim decided that this was his new calling, and after attending 155 executions, he resigned as a death row chaplain and took a job with Victim Services on the other side of the street. At the time, he had no idea just how big that relatively small move would prove.

"The first execution was very interesting to me. It was all pretty uneventful, but everything felt so different. On execution day, I usually took part in the preparations at the prison, but instead, I went over to the La Quinta Inn to meet the relatives. We told them what was happening and got them ready. There were two of us there, myself and my colleague Gene Stuart, who was my superior.

"We were friends; don't get me wrong, but Gene and I never really connected on a spiritual level. Still, he was in charge, so I just followed his lead. After talking to the relatives at the hotel, we drove over to the prison."

It was 5:00 p.m. by the time they arrived.

"It felt so strange to get there at the same time as a whole bunch of other people. I'd always been inside with the inmates, but now I was on the outside with a couple of media representatives and the grieving families, watching the whole thing. As they entered the prison, the relatives were searched. That was an unpleasant experience for everyone, and to make them feel a little more comfortable, we were searched, too. We made sure that always took place after that day so the relatives didn't feel like they were being singled out. And then we headed upstairs and prepared them a little more."

The execution was scheduled to begin at 6:00 p.m.

"It felt so strange and alien to me, heading in there at that time of evening, walking straight to the witness room, and seeing it from a completely different angle. I was so used to being on the other side. The witness room for the victim's relatives was pretty small, with just one large window. There was space for five people sitting side by side, and there were usually five relatives, Gene and me, a press representative, someone from the inspector's office, and a guard. It was cramped, to say the least."

As Jim made his way in and saw the inmate on the gurney, already strapped down, the knowledge of what had gone on in the execution chamber filled him with a sense of emptiness.

"I was jealous. I felt like a stranger; I guess that's the truth. I was no longer a part of the inner circle. I missed spending time with the inmate because there were so many things I couldn't do with the victim's family. I think that was the hardest part. With the prisoner, I could go in and talk with him and find out so much. We could discuss his faith and the execution process. With the prisoner, there was an end result. We talked, he died, and hopefully, he ended up in Heaven."

But with the victim's relatives, things were different.

"You have three hours with them at the hotel, and then you get into the car, drive to the prison, go inside, and watch someone die. After that, you drive back to the hotel and help them process the experience for as long as they want you there, then you say goodbye, and that's it. The whole thing felt so empty. With the prisoner, you prepared him for one specific moment, and when it eventually came around, that was the end for him. But with the victim's relatives, it was just the beginning. I wasn't with them when they really started going through the process. They went back to their lives, and I didn't mean a thing to them. Not that I think I'm important; that's not what I'm trying to say. But I lost out on the key part. Two weeks after the execution, I was supposed to call to check on them, but more than half didn't even pick up. It was frustrating not knowing how they were doing."

· · ·

When did you realize you'd made a mistake?

"That very first time."

And yet you stayed there for another 121 executions?

"Yes. I needed the job, and I couldn't just go back to my old one because they'd already appointed a new chaplain. I had integrity. I wasn't going to tell them to fire him because I wanted to come back. Larry, who took over from me, was a good friend of mine. But if he had ever quit, I would have returned. Looking back now, that was the worst mistake I ever made—and Lord knows I've made plenty. I loved the work. I loved the freedom of being able to spread the gospel. At Victim Services, I couldn't talk about God at all. My first boss there said I could, but once she left, the rules changed."

What did you think once you realized your mistake?

"Right there and then, my only thought was, 'What can I do to fix this?' I wanted to know how I could make the experience more meaningful for the victim's families. It just felt like there was so much they were missing out on."

For one, Jim didn't think the hotel was the right place for him to do his job. He couldn't get as close to the victims as he wanted there, so he got in touch with the First Baptist

Church in Huntsville to ask if he could use one of their rooms instead. The church agreed.

"The first time we went over there, they prepared a basket for us full of fruit, candy and drinks. One of their Sunday school classes presented it to the relatives. They took us through to a quiet room where we wouldn't be disturbed, which made a big difference. There was a TV and a VCR, and we showed them a short video about the process. The film itself wasn't all that informative—it was actually just a news item from Austin. Still, we showed it in an attempt to prepare them, but I never really felt like I got through."

Jim was never fully satisfied with the situation.

"There was just so little time for them to process what was about to happen because we had to wait until we had an execution date to contact them. Once that happened, we had to reach out to them by mail. Some called us back right away, and some waited, but the majority went into a state of shock as soon as the letter arrived. They often didn't know how to conduct themselves in that world, so we had to explain everything."

Jim was also only able to contact those relatives who had indicated in advance that they wanted to be present for the execution.

"We got in touch, and once they replied, we asked if they knew of anyone else who might want to be present and if they had their contact information. It was such a slow process."

Toward the end of Jim's career, the rules changed, and they were expected to contact all of the victim's relatives.

"That made our job so much harder because the execution often took place ten to fifteen years after the crime, and we had no idea where these people lived. Once the inmate was given a date, we had to work like dogs to find information about the victims' relatives. Some were already dead, some didn't care, and some got angry with us for contacting them. It was a tough gig, but that's how they do it to this day. They have to contact everyone, which makes it all so much more stressful—and no more useful than before."

It also made it much trickier from a numbers point of view because there was only space for five victims' relatives to observe the execution, regardless of how many wanted to be there.

"There was one man with over 100 victims, but the room only had space for five. How were we supposed to decide who got to be there? He was a serial killer, Tommy Lynn Sells. He wrote me a letter containing a list of 128 people he claimed to have killed. There were actually 165 in total, but he said he couldn't remember the names of the others. I didn't try to find out whether he was telling the truth or not. I showed the letter to a few people, but nothing came of it. He sent it to a newspaper, too."

Tommy Lynn Sells was only ever convicted of one murder—a thirteen-year-old girl he raped and then stabbed to death before slashing the throat of her ten-year-old friend. Miraculously, the latter survived and managed to identify him, and the police also found his fingerprints on the victim's body.

"That was how they got him. But there were no charges for any of the other deaths. The majority were in different states."

Jim first met Tommy Lynn Sells during a mediation session, back during his time as the prison chaplain.

"A woman requested it. She was from Mississippi, I

think. She wanted him to confess to killing her husband. They'd had a home invader, and her husband died. Everyone in her community blamed her despite the fact that there was no evidence she had done anything wrong. She'd called the cops, and they came out. The killer had stolen a few things, but he hadn't left any prints or other evidence. She asked Sells to confess to the murder, but that session was doomed to fail from the very start. I actually met him a few times after that, four or five in total. He was a real psychopath. When he spoke about the things he'd done, it was never to talk about the victims; he just wanted to brag about how he killed them."

Considering you'd been on the other side, you must have known some of the prisoners who were later executed?

"Yes, and the victims' relatives were aware of that. They knew I'd spent a long time working on the other side. I was actually familiar with the perpetrator in most of the executions. That made things a little trickier because the relatives were sometimes quite reserved toward me."

They didn't want anyone to say anything positive about the person they'd come to see die?

"Exactly. And as for me, I was so frustrated. I was stuck with a group of people I really couldn't help, and I knew that right there on the gurney was a man I could have talked to and prayed with. I could have preached to his family. It just felt like I'd been silenced."

What kind of expectations do the victims' relatives have when they go into the chamber to watch a person die? What do they imagine?

"You mean in terms of what would happen?"

Yes. My impression is that, in Sweden, where we don't have the death penalty, people have to grieve differently. Let's say someone kills one of my brothers. Once the trial is over, there's nothing left for me to do. With a bit of luck, the killer will get life in prison—which means a sentence of sixteen years. That's the maximum possible penalty. You can't get any more than that.

"Sixteen years is a life sentence?"

Yes, after sixteen years, or thereabouts, almost everyone is released—unless there are very special circumstances.

"Really?"

.   .   .

Yes. That's it. So, once the trial is over, that means I have to deal with myself. I have to finish grieving. I have to go through my own process. There's nothing more the courts or anyone else can do for me. I think people in Sweden grieve differently because there's no date ten years in the future where you can expect some sense of closure from watching someone die for their misdeeds. That just doesn't exist.

"You're right. The process is actually even worse than that if you really stop to think about it because once a person has been sentenced to death, they automatically get an appeal. That means that within just a short space of time, there could be a new investigation. For these people, the victims' relatives, the pain is so raw and real. They're terrified of some technicality coming to light, meaning the conviction will be overturned and the perpetrator set free. They're worried about him coming after them. There is so much fear and anxiety; it's one huge rollercoaster."

For many years, prisoners sentenced to death were able to appeal against their conviction as many times as they liked.

"It wasn't uncommon for them to make twenty different appeals over a twenty-year period. And every time an appeal is filed, the victim's family is forced to go through the whole process again. Up and down, up and down. They're emotional prisoners because everything is focused on the killer and not the victim. They're constantly grieving that. And then, when the perpetrator is finally given a date, they find themselves facing a whole host of difficult questions: Do I want to be there to watch this person die? Do I want to meet them? What will happen? Is there a risk he could hurt me while I'm in there? What about his relatives? Will they attack me? Many people were afraid of that. They didn't want to appear on TV or want anyone to see them in that situation."

My impression, as an outsider looking in, is that these people enter the witness room after being frozen for a decade or more, and they have this expectation that when they step into that room, they'll be freed from all these feelings. But what they actually find is that they only really start grieving then because they haven't processed their loss; they've been too focused on a hypothetical moment of death at some point in the future.

"They really are frozen in time. Fifteen, sixteen, sometimes as many as twenty-five years can pass, and they're just stuck. I can honestly say that, on execution day, the majority of the victims' relatives are still right where they were when their loved one died. No one has helped them to process their feelings. People often talk about the four stages of grief. It starts with shock, a surreal phase where the person has trouble processing the fact that their loved one is gone. That gives way to reaction, where feelings of desperation, fear, anger, and loss take over. The person who has lost someone can be totally overwhelmed by their grief, to the extent that they don't have the strength for anything else. Most of the people I meet on execution day are still in that phase. They haven't reached the processing stage yet, where they start to gain perspective on their loss and how it will affect the rest of their lives; they're still clinging onto the phase before that, where their thoughts keep going back to the perpetrator. As long as they get their punishment, they think, I can move on. But sadly, that isn't how it works. The last stage is the reorientation phase, where a person both can and wants to move on with their life. It isn't that they forget the person who died, but those feelings of loss no longer dominate. I think you probably reach that stage quicker in Sweden because you're not held back by the process in the same way we are here."

And is that what you thought you'd be able to do in this job? Help people reorient themselves?

"Yes, but that isn't how it worked out. I told you when we were talking about Alabama that the one thing I always heard from families following an execution was that it had been 'too easy.' That was probably what eighty percent of them said."

It's a shame they weren't in Alabama with Yellow Mama so they could see the killers fry.

"Yes, many of them would have preferred that."

In that case, the death penalty isn't really about justice at all. It's about revenge.

. . .

"A big part of it is revenge, yes. After saying that the execution was too easy, the relatives always added, 'But at least he's gone now, so he can't hurt anyone else.' There was one guy, Leo Jenkins, and when he was executed... No, I should wind back and tell you the full story. When he was executed, I was still a chaplain on death row. That was one of the first executions the victim's relatives were allowed to attend."

Why did they change the rules so the victim's family could be there?

"There was an intensive campaign from the victims' side, an organization called Parents of Murdered Children. They convinced the Texas Board of Criminal Justice to change the policy. I thought it was a great idea; I had no problem with it. They just split the large witness room in two by constructing a wall down the middle."

The prisoners weren't quite so positive, however.

"They didn't want them there—and understandably. Who wants the last thing they ever see to be a bunch of people who hate them? Leo Jenkins was the first to be executed following the change, which meant it was a big news story—the BBC actually came over to make a documentary about it. In connection with that, a group of people were shown around the Walls Unit, and I was asked to explain how everything worked. They wanted to see the execution chamber, so we went over to the death house, and I took them through the process. I remember them standing by the window and me by the gurney. I told them I always tried to bring the prisoner some sort of comfort during his last few minutes of life, and one of the women interrupted me to ask, 'What did you say you do?' I replied that, as a chaplain, it was my job to prepare the inmates to meet God."

Leo Jenkins had killed two siblings, a brother and a sister, at the pawnbroker's shop they ran together. He was high on drugs at the time, and he had also confessed to his crime some years earlier.

"It turned out the woman who asked the question was the murdered siblings' mother. She said, 'Hold on a second. You're telling me you come in here and try to get them to become religious so that they end up in Heaven?' She paused for a few seconds before saying, 'I don't want you in here with him. How dare you? How dare you believe that God, my God, would let this murderer walk the same streets as my children in Heaven?'

"I replied that I was sorry she felt that way but that it was my job to do just that. The woman said, 'No, I don't want you in here,' and that was the end of my conversation with her."

They left the execution chamber and moved on, but Jim was hurt that someone wanted to stop him from doing his job.

He saw the woman again a few days later at Leo Jenkins' execution.

"I saw her through the window, but we didn't interact."

Did you put your hand on his ankle?

• • •

259

"Yes, I did. It was about giving him a sense of comfort at a difficult moment."

Did you look up at her as you did it?

"No, I tried to... I concentrated on him. That was where my focus was, on him, because that was my job. She was on the other side."

Could you understand her anger?

"Sure. I can definitely understand it, but theologically, I can't agree with it."

Do you believe he ended up in the same place as her children?

"He asked for forgiveness and told me he was Christian."

So, you think they're in the same place, Leo Jenkins and the siblings he killed?

"I don't know where the siblings are. I don't know if they were Christian; they didn't attend church. Most people assume that their nearest and dearest automatically go to

Heaven when they die. Even the ones without any kind of relationship with God hope that their children will go to Heaven. In the BBC documentary that was broadcast afterward, the woman talked about the execution and said the words I'd heard so often before: It was too easy. He didn't suffer anywhere near as much as my children. She made that statement at their grave the day after the execution. She said, 'I'm so glad it's over. He can't harm anyone else now. He was using air someone else could've been breathing.' And that's where the documentary ended."

What did you make of that?

"That it was probably a little harsh. Her words stayed with me, though—about Leo Jenkins being a waste of air. He was terrified, and he had opened his heart to Christ. We spoke about his victims. He knew what he had done and the damage he had caused, but there was nothing he could do to undo that."

Did you tell him about your meeting with the mother?

"No, because if I had mentioned it to him and he had turned around in the chamber and said something to her, that could have led to a real fuss in the press. Does that make sense?"

. . .

Yes. One thing I've been wondering about is what made you decide to put a hand on their ankle as they died?

"It was Leo Jenkins. That very evening, in fact."

He was the first person you did that with?

"He was the first. That evening in the death house, as he was strapped to the table, he said, 'It feels so lonely up here.' They were busy trying to insert the IV line at the time. He said, 'It feels like there's no one else here,' so I asked the warden if I could put a hand on his leg. He said I could, so I did just that, right above his ankle. And he said, 'That's better. Now, I'm not alone.' That made me feel good."

Did you do it every time after that?

"I always asked them first. I said, 'Do you want me to put a hand on your leg?' There were only three people I didn't ask."

Gary Graham, Ponchai Wilkerson, and Juan Soria?

"Correct."

Chapter Seventeen

People have changed. Everyone just thinks of themselves nowadays.

2001

One day in early spring, the phone rang in Jim's office, as it often did. A woman's voice asked him to hold, and a moment later, a man came onto the line. He introduced himself as a federal judge in New York and said that the state was preparing to carry out its first execution in years. They wanted to organize a conference to investigate the impact the death penalty might have on their staff, and the judge asked Jim to be one of the speakers.

"I explained that I basically just go in and talk to people

about Jesus, and he said, 'Well, come up here and talk to us about Jesus, then.'"

Jim said he would be happy to. The warden gave him the green light, and he flew to New York for the first time in his life.

"It was incredible. It was March 17, St. Patrick's Day, and we stood on the steps outside St. Patrick's Cathedral and watched the parade.... Oh, it was a wonderful day."

I've been there for that, too. It's a good day to be in New York City.

"It really is. All the bagpipes... I loved every minute of it. Then, I got a chance to speak to all the lawyers there and share my experiences with them. The day after that, I went to the *New York Times* to be interviewed by one of their reporters. I also went to the World Trade Center to visit the FBI offices there. I spent the whole day with the FBI, just talking about God. They were very receptive to everything I had to say. I got to visit the very top of the World Trade Center, too. To walk about up there. It was unbelievable. Just six months later, it would be gone."

What do you remember of 9/11?

"Every single minute of it. I remember exactly where I was when I heard the news. I was in my office, the chaplain's office, and we had a TV in our meeting room. Someone came in and said, 'There's been an attack in New York,' and so I ran to the TV to see what was going on; everyone did. We were completely paralyzed. No one was getting any work done, so in the end, everyone who was able to took the day off. We spent three days glued to the TV. What a tragedy. During my visit to the World Trade Center, I actually became good friends with a guy from the FBI. It took a while, but I eventually managed to make contact with him. He called me to let me know he was safe. He said, 'I can't tell you where I am, but thank you for your prayers.' He could feel that I had been praying for him."

NOVA, the National Organization for Victim Assistance, had Jim on its list of stand-by volunteers in case of emergency. After 9/11, he got a call asking him to go to Washington, D.C. He drove up there all the way from Huntsville—a journey of almost 1,400 miles, which took him twenty-one hours.

"When we arrived at the Pentagon, I assumed it would be a long process to actually get inside the area, but it wasn't at all. I just walked around and was there for anyone who wanted to talk. We stood mostly and talked to people in the security shack close to the entrance. There were people in tears all over the place. The building was still smoking, and the stench of jet fuel was still hanging in the air. Seeing the terrible thing that had happened, knowing how many lives had been lost, it was just so overwhelming."

One of the men he met, Craig Sincock, worked at the Pentagon—as had Cheryle, his wife of twenty-five years.

"I take it you've seen pictures of where the plane hit? The point where the nose of the airplane struck was her office. They never found a single trace of her; she was just gone. Being able to sit down and talk with Craig, pray with him, and help him through the grieving process meant a lot. I felt honored to be able to talk to the people who had been there."

A year later, Jim was invited to a NOVA conference in Nashville, Tennessee, and as he walked into the hotel lobby, he bumped into the same man: Craig Sincock.

"We got to talking, and he told me that he had started an organization called the Pentagon Angels, a survivor group for people who worked there. It felt good to know he had moved on. It was a gift from God to be able to meet him again under different circumstances."

Jim had never been to the capital before and ended up staying in Washington, D.C., for two weeks.

"Even now, I get emotional when I think about it. There was a no-fly zone in place at the time, which meant there was nothing in the sky, not a single plane anywhere. It was such a chaotic period. I remember walking down the Mall to the water, looking at the reflections. I walked between the Lincoln Memorial and the Washington Memorial, and a bunch of military helicopters flew overhead. That was the only thing you ever saw in the air. It was strange, knowing that the world was changing, that these helicopters weren't flying where they were supposed to be. It worried me, but it also brought me a feeling of peace. I don't know how to explain it, but I felt God's presence in a very real sense when I saw all those people gathered. Right after the attacks, churches started filling up again; everyone had re-discovered their faith, and people were flying the American flag on their cars and at their homes. That was refreshing to see. It made me hope that what happened wasn't the end of the world after all, that we had a chance for a new start."

. . .

Did you think 9/11 was the end of the world?

"Yes, I did. Or maybe not the end of the world as such, but the end of the world as I knew it. I assumed there would be more to come, that we would go to war, and that there would be bombs and explosions everywhere. That's what I thought."

Jim has clear memories of that day.

"I remember the planes flying into the towers. I can still see the footage of the second one hitting. Such devastation, suddenly compounded by the second plane, by not knowing who was responsible or why it was happening, and then we heard about Pennsylvania and the Pentagon, and our safe little world wasn't so safe anymore. It felt like a really dangerous place."

Which part of the Bible do you associate with 9/11?

"At the time, my answer definitely would have been the Book of Revelation because of the pain and the suffering, the end, the devastation to come. Toward the end of the Book of Revelation, in chapters sixteen, seventeen, and eighteen, there's a section about the fall of Babylon and how the demons will be used to destroy Babylon, the harlot, and how God is instrumental in crushing her because people had turned their back on Him. But the fact that I was able to visit New York and preach about God there gave me a different perspective."

Jim believes that 9/11 can be compared to the fall of Babylon.

"I think it was a warning to us. America is so blessed, and yet we have turned away from the word of God. We compromise the word of God—and I'm talking about churches and Christians here, not just unbelievers. We've taken God for granted, and in my opinion, 9/11 should have been a wake-up call to us, a reminder that we need to stand close to God."

Was God involved in what happened? Was it a punishment?

"I don't believe that God hit the start button, but I do believe He let it happen. I really do think that what happened was incredibly important for America. It was definitely a wake-up call to me and a lot of other folks, but not quite loud enough."

So, what do you think should have happened after 9/11?

"We should have gone back to our roots, to our foundation as a Christian nation—even if we are an accommodating place where everyone has the right to their own faith and their own religion. The USA was founded on religious freedom, not freedom from religion. I hoped more people would realize that humans are not the highest power and that we need to go back to what really matters in life and stop being so narcissistic. But people have changed. Everyone just thinks of themselves nowadays."

. . .

Do you think, biblically speaking, that there was a reason the attacks focused on Washington and New York, or was that just down to the terrorists?

"I think it was down to the terrorists. If you read the Book of Revelation, it talks about Babylon and her evil, about people being blinded by the harlot—that's what she's called in scripture. It talks about the worlds that have been blinded by her charms and the fact that she has sex with all these men, but the key part is the immorality that brings about. It's not just about sex; it's about greed and power. Babylon focuses on what the *world* has to offer rather than what *God* has to offer. An angel took a millstone and threw it into the ocean, and with that, the city came crashing down. All the lights went out. The music stopped, and the irresponsibility ceased. There was no more laughter, no more weddings. The city was ruined. Evil had destroyed evil, and God let it happen. He didn't destroy it Himself; he used evil against evil. I think that could well be prophetic for the United States."

Would you say any of this to Craig Sincock, given his wife was one of those who died in Washington?

"Yes, I absolutely would."

. . .

And would you understand if he found it offensive that you were implying his wife was evil and needed to be destroyed?

"Oh, no! No, no, that's not how I see it at all. I'm not saying his wife was evil. The passage in the Bible goes something like, 'Rejoice, for God has avenged you on Babylon.' There was evil in the city, but none of those who died were evil. They're victims, and if you look at chapter 19 of the Book of Revelation, it talks about rejoicing because God has avenged you. He destroyed Babylon because Babylon has taken you, and of course, it talks about those in Heaven who lost their lives because of their faith—the true martyrs."

Do you think of the people who died on 9/11 as martyrs?

"No, I don't. I see them as victims."

Jim gets up to fetch his Bible. The plan was to turn to the Book of Revelation, but in the end, we read through the first few pages, which are full of messages to him from death row inmates.

"Steven Renfro. He was the first person to be executed after Karla Faye, and I've already told you that she was the first to write in this book. As he ate his last meal, he asked me whether we were sitting in the same place Karla Faye Tucker had sat. I said that we were, that she had sat on the very same bunk as him. He was quiet for a while, and then he asked how I thought she had felt at that moment. I remembered she had written in my Bible, so I showed him her words. Reading them, he got tears in his eyes and asked whether he could write something, too. He wrote, 'Dear Pastor Jim, thank you for the comfort you provided in my time of need. God bless you. Jesus is Lord. Your friend, Steven.' I think he wrote that exactly a week after Karla Faye. It was very calm that day with none of the fuss we'd had when she was executed. Lots of inmates started writing messages after that. I never asked them to. All these greetings were their own initiative."

Do you have a favorite?

"Hmm. Karla Faye's is probably my favorite. Seeing their words brings back so many memories and feelings—sadness, in some ways. You see all these lives, and you think of the countless others who died as a result of their actions. It's all just so sad."

He points to the Bible.

"Right there, in the middle."

It reads: "I have walked in the wild of Satan and walked with the grace of God, but I have never felt more at peace with the Lord as I feel now sitting in this death watch cell after talking to the ones around me and have been blessed with love and forgiveness of my Creator and look forward to the moment I am with him."

"Excell White wrote that. He was the one who spent the longest on death row, who had the same shoes for twenty-five years."

. . .

You say that looking at these messages makes you feel sad, but does it ever make you think about the death penalty itself?

"No, I try to steer clear of that discussion. All I see is death, and that's what I look at. When I worked in a hospital during my studies, people died, and there was nothing I could do about it. I just wanted to make a difference to them, and I had to take the same approach with these prisoners. There was no politics. There was no right or wrong. They were there, and they were going to die, and I wanted to make sure they were as prepared for that moment as they could be."

I forgot to ask: did Bobbie go with you to Washington and New York?

"She came to New York. I stayed in one hotel, and she was in another, but we did a little sightseeing together. I didn't think it was appropriate to share a room, given that we weren't married."

Chapter Eighteen

As a Christian, I've never been afraid of death.
It's what you have to go through to get to that point that
scares me.

By early 2002, Jim felt as though his life had come to a standstill. He was unhappy in his job, missed being a chaplain, and his relationship wasn't working.

"I'd spent years asking Bobbie to be my wife, but she didn't want to get married. It was a relationship without a future. She just kept on saying she didn't want to, and by June, it got to the point where I couldn't take any more. I asked her to marry me one last time, but she said no."

Jim told Bobbie that if she didn't want to marry him, he would have no choice but to move on because the life they were living wasn't right for him. He was fifty years old, and he didn't want to start over with someone else at that stage of his life, but he would have to end their relationship if she was really sure. With a brief 'Okay,' they parted ways.

Around this time, Jim also found out that his brother Tom had been diagnosed with leukemia.

"He served in Vietnam, which meant he was exposed to Agent Orange and that kind of thing. We assumed that must be one of the reasons he was affected. He was really sick for a while, but he started chemotherapy right away, which eased his symptoms a little."

A few months passed. Jim had given Bobbie a key to his apartment before they broke up, and she had never given it back. As he was sleeping one day, he woke to the sound of the front door opening and assumed someone must have broken in. He sat up in bed and saw Bobbie in the doorway. Jim asked what she was doing there, and she said they needed to talk.

"I scooted over to make room for her, and she sat beside me and said, 'I miss you, and I miss us.' I said, 'I miss you too, but I can't spend the rest of my life waiting for you because I don't want to live in sin. I loved you then, and I love you now, and I could marry you right this instant.'"

Bobbie said okay.

They got married in November of that year. Jim has

never asked what made her change her mind or what she did during their time apart.

"All that matters is that she's here and that she came back to me."

Getting married for the second time proved completely different from the first.

"We got married in a small county church not far from New Waverly. It wasn't our usual church, but the setting was so beautiful. I really liked it, so they let us have the ceremony there. It took place on November 30. Bobbie's mom lived in Columbus, Ohio, and she had come down to visit. Bobbie wanted her to be there for the wedding, so we brought everything forward. There were so many guests: workmates, friends, all our kids and grandkids."

The next morning, they went to church and then drove to Branson, Missouri, for their honeymoon—in separate cars.

"Bobbie drove with her mom, and I followed in my car. We all slept in the same room."

You, your new wife, and your mother-in-law?

"Yes, she stayed in the same room as us. We couldn't afford two."

Haha. Very romantic.

"It probably wasn't how I would've wanted it, but that's how it was. Bobbie's mom had always dreamed of seeing The

Rockettes, the dance company from Radio City Music Hall in New York, and when we found out they were doing a show in Branson, we headed over there and spent three days with my mother-in-law in a hotel."

Do you think this marriage will last until death do you part?

"As far as I'm concerned, it will. I said until death do us part, and I meant it. When I married Bobbie she became my best friend, my soul mate and supporter. I thank God for her every day. If she wants to leave me, that's her decision, but I'll never leave Bobbie. She's someone who listens, who doesn't judge, and she likes to do and see things. But more than anything, I love her because she loves me—and God. She's a hard worker. An organizer. Probably a little OCD. I'm with the person I need to be with."

As he says those words, Bobbie comes into the room to tell us she has made lunch. She laughs at his description of her as being a little OCD.

"I'm with the person I need to be with, too," she says as she turns to leave.

In early 2003, Jim's brother Tom found out that his leukemia was back, and he underwent another round of chemotherapy.

"It helped some, but the doctors told him they weren't sure how much longer they would be able to continue giving him that treatment."

Not long later, Jim discovered a lump at the top of his neck, just beneath his right ear.

"It really hurt for a while, and then it didn't hurt at all, but it didn't go away. Ultimately, I went to see my doctor, who said I needed to have it removed. He cut it out and said he would call me once he had the test results, but I never heard from him. My ear started getting painful again, so I went to see him, and he said, 'There's something not right here.' He poked about in my ear a little, and then I left. I'd only gotten as far as the Woodlands Mall when my phone rang. It was the doctor, and he said, 'Mr. Brazzil, I just got the biopsy results. You have leukemia.'"

He told you over the phone?

"Yes, that was a little upsetting. It's not the kind of news you want to be given over the phone, especially when you were only there fifteen minutes ago. Anyway, I called my brother that evening and said, 'Tom, tell me about this leukemia business.' He asked why, and I said, 'Because I have it too.'"

The same kind?

"The exact same kind. Stage four lymphocytic leukemia. It's a chronic lymphoma."

The fact that both brothers had the same form of cancer made the doctors want to study them, but sadly, there was no time for that. Tom passed away in 2004.

"That left a real void in my heart because we were very close."

To Jim, it was also a death sentence.

"The doctor told me I would have five good years before things went downhill, but that my leukemia was very slow-growing. That didn't faze me because I'd already received one death sentence when I was ten. As a Christian, I've never been afraid of death. It's what you have to go through to reach that point that scares me. I don't want to suffer. I don't want to become a burden on anyone. I don't want to have to go to the toilet in a bedpan. I don't want to be full of tubes. I don't want that sort of life. I don't want to end up in a hospice and have to lie there waiting for someone to come in and sponge me down or give me shots. That's not what I want. No, death isn't something I'm afraid of. I just pray that God doesn't allow me to go through all that toward the end."

Would you welcome help in dying?

"No. On a purely selfish level, yes, because I don't want to suffer, but so long as I can still breathe, I believe that God has a plan for me, and I don't want to take that away from Him. It has been tempting at times, but as Paul says, 'For to me to live is Christ, and to die is gain.'"

It was the third round of chemotherapy that ultimately killed his brother, but with Jim, the doctors took a different approach. They gave him just one round of chemo made up of a cocktail of two different drugs.

"It took them ten hours to give me the drip, so they sedated me for the duration. I loved it. I slept like a baby for ten hours, and when I woke up, it was done. After that, I took pills for twenty-one days, followed by a break, then got started with another drip. We repeated that process for six months, and it slowed the growth. It's still growing, but slowly."

During his treatment, Jim continued to work for Victim Services.

In 2005, Hurricane Katrina hit. The storm swept through the Dayton area, leaving the women's prison without power. Jim was asked to go over there to try to calm the inmates, see what the situation was like, and work alongside the staff who had been there around the clock. It was a difficult situation, and they had been without running water for days on end.

"That meant the inmates couldn't shower or flush the toilets. A bunch of porta-potties had been delivered—I think they had around 180 of them there—but they were in desperate need of clothes and shoes because it was the middle of winter, and everyone was freezing. The staff had ordered winter clothing but were sent a whole load of tongue depressors instead. Whenever I see one of those now, I always find myself thinking back to that time."

Jim went to speak to the warden, who broke down in tears the minute he stepped into her office. She was exhausted. Communication with Huntsville was near impossible because the phone lines were down, and she had so many decisions to make. She told him that she wasn't sure how much more she would be able to take.

"She said, 'We've got two thousand women here, many of whom are on their period, but we have no tampons and no running water. It's been days since anyone last took a shower, and the smell of their bodies....' She said it was the worst thing she had ever been through, and then she cried and cried. I tried to talk to her, held her hand, and listened."

The lack of power meant that the prison's security doors weren't working as usual, and the women had no choice but to stay in their cells. As a result, Jim couldn't gather them for prayer or sermons.

"The doors could be operated manually, so I did go to see each of them, one after another. There was a rancid stench of old blood, urine, and feces about the place, all mixed together; it really was terrible—probably the worst thing I ever smelled. Seeing women in prison... I don't know how to explain it, but I always felt more uneasy in women's facilities than I did in men's. When you speak to a man, you can just talk to him and try to reason with him. On the whole, it's possible to calm a man down. But with a woman, you have to be more emotional. And all these young women in prison, they're so unpredictable. You can tell when it's their time of the month—when they're angry and in pain and feel lonely and desperate. They can be dangerous."

Dangerous? Were you really afraid?

"Yes, on one occasion in particular. There was this big woman there, and she was so angry. She started throwing things around as I tried to talk to her, and it just got worse and worse. I stopped talking and backed away, just let her scream and shout until the guards arrived to take over. As I said earlier, treat someone like an animal, and they'll start behaving like one."

The five years of Jim's second death sentence came and went. He continued to work for Victim Services, and though he still didn't like the job, it did pay the bills. He certainly had plenty. In fact, Jim is still paying off his cancer treatment today even though he had health insurance via the prison.

"Not everything about it was bad. My colleagues and I got to take a lot of courses. We did one with the International Critical Incident Stress Foundation, for example, and ended up becoming instructors with them. We traveled to Baltimore, came back here, and started a program called Crisp. We took that all around Texas, teaching prison staff how to deal with people in crisis. I took a lot of satisfaction from that; I really did enjoy it. Doing that also meant I got away from the victim side of executions for a long time. That was a welcome break because I think I was probably burnt out; I really wasn't doing well."

In 2012, Jim was diagnosed with prostate cancer.

"I was having trouble peeing, so I went to a urologist who gave me a regular prostate exam. My PSA levels were high, and they took a biopsy and found the cancer. I spoke to a surgeon about removing it, but he didn't recommend it; he said it wasn't worth the risk and that I should have a lot of sex instead. That's good for the prostate, apparently. When I got home and told Bobbie that day, she was angry. 'So, I'm expected to step up now, am I?' she asked. I told her that I didn't expect her to do anything. I've reached a stage in my life where I don't love people because of what they do for me; I love them for who they are. And Bobbie has no interest in sex these days."

As though by magic, Bobbie comes into the room at that exact moment. She asks, 'How y'all doing?' and I tell her that we were just talking about how she has no interest in sex. She glances over at her husband, then sits down beside him on the sofa and says that the sex was great at first but that a woman's body changes after menopause. I tell them that they should continue this discussion later, without me and my tape recorder, and with that, she gets up and leaves the room.

With Jim fighting two different types of cancer, he decided that something had to give. He had done more than enough for the Texas Department of Criminal Justice.

"I was tired, and I was hurting. I was sixty-two, and I'd been working for the state for twenty years. I was no longer allowed to pray with the victims. I couldn't talk about God. I had to be sensitive to society rather than the will of the Lord. That wasn't what I signed up for, and I realized I could no longer do much good there. I was burnt out. I'd spent twenty years on an emotional rollercoaster because of that job."

He retired in March 2012.

"I went through a grieving process; I really did. I was ready to leave Victim Services, but I missed my work at the prison. I had such ambivalent feelings toward that job within the correctional system. I was happy and felt so blessed, but I was also frustrated by the knowledge that I could have done so much more. I felt as though I'd let them down on that front. But looking back now, I know I did what I could within the limited area I had access to."

Shortly after his retirement, Jim was also diagnosed with Sjögren's Syndrome, an autoimmune disease.

"It's a little like lupus. Dry mouth and dry eyes, but it affects all the organs and attacks them. Sometimes you feel just fine, and then it'll hit a specific organ and knock it out before moving on to the next."

Will it eventually kill you?

"The Sjögren's? No. It's the other two that will kill me."

Chapter Nineteen

They accepted me, and I really hadn't expected to be accepted.

2012-2019

As Jim's time in the prison system was coming to an end, he heard from a friend who occasionally filled in as a preacher.

"He asked if I would be interested in helping out at a small church in the town of Weldon because he couldn't make it there every Sunday. I said I would be happy to, but that I needed him to prepare the congregation and tell them I was divorced. 'Me too,' he said, and that was that."

The first time Jim drove over there, he was struck by just how beautiful the journey from Huntsville was. It took him across the Trinity River and past tall, handsome pines. For once, his mind wasn't on all the prisons he passed along the way.

"I love pines. They were one of the things I liked most about Huntsville. And then I remember driving past the Eastham Unit and thinking, 'This is new. Today is a new day.' I pulled up in the parking lot outside the church and saw that there were only two or three other cars there. That was a little disappointing because I had been hoping for more. Still, I went in, and it all felt so welcoming and loving."

There were seven people there that day, just as there had been in his very first church.

"No one was wearing a tie. The women were nicely dressed, and so were the men—in khakis and shirts—but they weren't dressed up. That small group gave me the self-confidence I needed because they accepted me, and I really hadn't expected to be accepted. I started out by telling them that there was something they needed to know, and then I said I was divorced. I didn't blame it on Janice; I just said that there were irreconcilable differences between us and that she was the one who had wanted to end our marriage. I said, 'I accept whatever you have to say about that; I just wanted you to know.' One of the men there said, 'That belongs in the past.' And then I gave them a sermon."

When do you plan to stop feeling guilty about being divorced?

"There's a passage in the First Epistle to Timothy that covers the demands placed on a man of the Church, 'A deacon must be the husband of but one wife.' But I've been married twice."

· · ·

Not anytime soon, by the sounds of it?

"I guess not."

That was the first time in almost twenty years that Jim had delivered a sermon in church.

"Other than at my relatives' funerals, that is. I was nervous, so nervous. There was a lot of uncertainty surrounding the whole thing, but I was also excited. I was doing something I thought I would never be able to do again: preach in a church in the free world. I had resigned myself to the idea that the only pastoral work I would ever be able to do was in prison. But now that I'd been given a second chance, I felt more empowered to do God's work than I ever had when I was a pastor full-time. I was less afraid of the consequences, too."

He tells me there was a thirst for the word of God in that little church in Weldon, Texas.

"They had an even greater longing for it than the inmates did. They blessed me more than I blessed them."

Because he was no longer an employee of the state, Jim and Bobbie had to leave the house included as a perk of the job within the Texas Corrections System, but the new congregation had a solution for that. One of the men offered to build them a house on his own land.

"He gave us full access to 200 acres, all to ourselves. I really couldn't have found a better place to serve God. Those years were wonderful."

By 2019, however, the cancer and the preaching had started to take their toll. Jim gave three sermons a week, on Sunday morning and Sunday and Wednesday evenings, and he began to notice that his voice was no longer holding up.

"Before I got to the end of my sermon, my voice would give out, and I couldn't finish. That kept happening, and I realized it was no good for anyone. They needed more than I could give, so I told Bobbie I had no choice but to quit. She suggested giving it another six months to see if things got any better, and I went along with that, but it only got worse. In the end, I just had to throw in the towel."

It proved hard to quit, however. By the time Jim left the church in Weldon, the congregation had grown tenfold to seventy people.

"I loved those people, and they loved me—loved us. I always used to call them... Do you remember the island full of odd toys in the animated film *Rudolph the Red-Nosed Reindeer and the Island of Misfit Toys?*"

Afraid not.

"Those people in Weldon, they didn't fit in anywhere else. They were a breed apart—country folks. They had their own philosophy: 'Shoot, shovel, or shut up.' And that was pretty much how things worked there. Leaving them was like leaving my own family."

Chapter Twenty

No matter how hard you try to control your own life,
you aren't the one in control, and you never will be.

2019-2022

Yet again, Jim found himself leaving a job that not only provided an income but a home. Fortunately, the answer to where life would take him next came in a phone call.

"My uncle—who was called Tom, just like my brother— had been asking me to come and live with him for years. He was ninety-seven when I retired from the church in Weldon, and Bobbie and I decided to move to Dallas to take care of him."

However, in the spring of 2021, Tom Bratcher died just a few days short of his ninety-ninth birthday.

"He left the house to us. For the first time in all our years together, we suddenly had a place we could really call home."

I ask whether they are happy in Dallas.

Both miss the countryside and their eighty-hectare plot, but one of the advantages of living in the city is that they are close to the seven specialists now keeping on top of Jim's health issues. He has recently started a new round of chemotherapy.

"I take four pills a day, and so far, it seems to be helping. They tell me that if the pills stop working, that's it for me."

Are you ready for that?

Sitting in his recliner chair, surrounded by Christmas decorations—though Bobbie claims most of them are still in storage—he laughs.

"There's an old saying that goes, 'I'm paid up, prayed up, packed up, and ready to go.' Whenever God is ready, I'm ready. But until I know that He is ready, I'll do all I can to continue the same fight."

How many people would you say are now in Heaven rather than Hell purely because you managed to change something in them? Off the top of your head.

"Around 1,500."

· · ·

Really? That's a lot.

"Mmhmm. Yes."

What will it be like to see them again up there?

"I think it'll be fun."

Who are you most looking forward to seeing up in Heaven?

"Oh, so many people. But I'll say, Troy Farris."

The man you baptized with a cup of water in his cell? Why him?

"I want to be able to say, 'Aren't you glad you found God's love? Just a few minutes before you died, you found the Lord, and now you have eternal life.' To me, that will be so satisfying."

Don't you think it's telling that of the 1,500 or so people you've helped reach Heaven, the one you most want to see again is a murderer?

"Troy Farris fought for so long because he was convinced he would never be forgiven. There was so much hatred and anger in his heart. To me, it was a powerful experience to see him realize that God still loved him that day—no matter what he'd done or how bad his sins were—and that God's love was powerful enough to forgive him. So, yes, I'd love to go up there and see him, even though my whole family is up there, too—my mom, dad and brother and others. I think Troy is among them because he finally opened his eyes before it was too late, and he gave his heart to Christ. And I was there to see that."

Or you helped him to do it?

"I might have said a few things, but it was God who did the hard work."

We've covered your whole life during our conversations. How do you feel about that now?

"I already told you that I think I probably need therapy for PTSD after all this."

He lets out another of the laughs I've grown used to during our time together.

"In all seriousness, though, I see how many opportunities

I have been given. There are so many gifts from the Lord where He said, 'Okay, I'll give you another chance. I'll help you. I forgive you.' It's a little like a young child brushing themselves off after a fall and getting right back up again. Life has never been boring. I've let God down in many ways, but He has always forgiven me, and once I die, I will make the journey home to be with Our Father. I'll have a new body, one free from all pain—I'm so sick of being in pain —and I will be with Him. I think I'll be at peace—that I'll get to rest."

What would you like people to say if someone were to ask who Jim Brazzil was?

"What do I want people to say about me? I want them to say without hesitation that he was a man of God, that he served his God. He might not always have done it well, but he served Him all the same. He was sincere in his faith. He was sincere in everything he tried to do. I think I have been. I want to be like Paul. I want to be able to say that I fought the good fight and that I've finished the race, and now the crown of righteousness awaits me—and not just me but anyone who believes in God. I've seriously considered officiating at my own funeral."

Do you mean recording a sermon for the service?

"Yes."

. . .

What would you say?

"Don't make the same mistakes I made. Don't turn away from God and become so conceited and self-assured that you think you can do everything on your own. You need Him with you."

Let's imagine for a moment that this is your funeral. I'm sitting among the other mourners. You get up and make your way to the front.

"I'd say that there are many lessons to be learned from all the problems in life. The first is that God loves you unconditionally. He loves you just the way you are, but He also wants you to let Him in. He wants to melt your heart. He wants to forgive you. He wants you to live a pure life. I would say that you should never become so self-sufficient that you no longer need Him. You can't do it all on your own. No matter how hard you try to control your own life, you aren't the one in control, and you never will be. There comes a time when you have to let go and allow God to take over. I learned that many times, particularly at executions. When a person had that needle in their arm, I always said it was down to them whether they made things easy or difficult. Once you feel the drugs start to take effect, don't fight it. Just let it happen. That's how I see God, too. Don't fight Him. Don't resist Him. Let Him in. Let Him make a difference in your life.

293

Just let Him happen. That's what I would say to you."

How does your body feel? Is it trying to shut down?

"It wants to shut down. I'm fighting all the time; I really am. It would be so easy for me just to lie down and let death come. I'm convinced that if I stopped fighting, it would be quick. But I don't feel ready yet. God can still make use of me. I'm trying not to pay any attention to time. All I have is today."

I notice that you still have dreams. When we went to the church with Bobbie and my husband yesterday, you said, 'Wow, I'd love to preach in this church.'

"Yes, but it was a mega-church with four thousand members. I've never preached to that many people before. It would be great to spread the word of God to thousands of people."

There was a great atmosphere, I'll give you that. The gospel choir gave both my husband and me goosebumps.

"That happens to me every time I hear them sing. What a gift to be able to touch people like that with your voice."

.   .   .

That's what you've done, too, in some ways.

"Ha. Thank you. Yes, I'd love to preach there. I'm always looking for new opportunities to do things. That fire is still burning. Right now, I don't have the energy to be a spiritual guide in a church, but there are other things I could do. Bible study, for example. We've spoken about organizing something like that here, in our lounge—holding Bible study groups here on Sunday mornings. Two of the neighbors have actually asked us to. Physically, I don't feel up to it yet, but I'm working on it."

I think it's time to wrap things up here. How do you feel now that our conversations are over?

"Scared."

Why?

"Because I've told you things I never told anyone else."

How was that for you?

"Hard. Laying myself bare like this is never easy. I don't feel comfortable talking about myself. I love talking about the things I've been through, but not myself."

Jim is quiet for a moment.

"Maybe you should wait until I'm dead to publish this book."

I don't know why it feels so important to have a record of this, but I glance down to make sure the Dictaphone is still running. I then turn to him in the brown leather recliner where he has spent hour after hour, day after day, surrounded by the decorations his wife has put up. There are nine faux Christmas trees of varying sizes in this room alone.

What makes you say that?

He looks up at the wooden cross on the wall—an object he has told me several times now was made by a prisoner—and hesitates for a moment before he answers.

"I'm a man of God. The confidences I've broken, the things I've done, everything I told you... I'm not sure how people will feel about all that. I just think it might be for the best if I'm not around when it comes out."

Are you afraid I might hurt you with what I write?

"I'm not afraid of you hurting me because I don't think you'll write anything I didn't say, but I'm afraid that the things I've told you will hurt others."

.   .   .

I think that sort of thing is in the eye of the beholder. Not everyone who reads this book will say, "Great work, Jim." But I think that some of the people who read it will gain insights that could change their lives.

"I'd be happy with that. What will be will be, I guess. I haven't told you anything that isn't true."

And I no longer feel quite so angry, just by the by.

"Well, hallelujah!"
    We both laugh.

Maybe there's a warrior in me after all.

"There's a warrior in all of us. We just need to find it."

The first time we spoke, you said that you always used to tell the dying people you met, "Thank you for sharing your life with me."

"That's right."

Thank you for sharing your life with me, Jim.

. . .

"You're welcome. I think life is there to be shared."

Afterword

A year has passed since our last meeting. It's January 2023, and Stockholm is buried beneath a thick layer of snow. In Dallas, where Jim still lives, it's a comparatively balmy fifty-one degrees.

I've tried to reach him several times over the past few days and feel a niggling anxiety creeping in. There have been so many times when I thought we might be saying goodbye for the last time. But now, as the phone rings and rings, I feel a rising sense of panic that we aren't done yet.

Is anyone ever really done?

Jim believes that we are, that he has said all he needs to say—to his family, to God, and to me.

He has given me his life's story to take care of as best I can—his memories—his experiences. Some of the people he has met along the way may remember things differently, and his words might cause them pain. But that wasn't his intention, nor is it mine.

Have I been clear enough with him that he changed my life? That our conversations about forgiveness—which all seemed so flat at first—sowed a seed in me? Have I told him how much less anger I carry inside me today than on the day we first met and how good that feels? Have I told him that there are days when I think about my father and experience a powerful longing to sit down and talk with him? I don't know whether something like that will ever happen, but it's good to think about my dad without seeing red. I wonder whether I ever told Jim how great it is that the weight on my chest is now mostly gone.

That isn't all down to a dying pastor from Texas, but my conversations with Jim Brazzil have definitely been a piece of the bigger puzzle.

I pick up the phone, fully expecting to hear the answering machine again.

But this time, he answers.

I tell him how glad I am that he is still here.

Jim laughs and says that it would have been a good day to die but that it was an even better day to live.

Thank you

Dear Jim, You changed my life in so many ways. Thank you to you and Bobbie for wanting your story to be told and for your honesty during this soul-searching process for both of us. I hope that this book, where you are in no way a hero, still shows my love and respect for you.

Thank you to Alice Menzies for doing a great job translating this book from Swedish. A big thank you to all the people at Forum Publishing House in Sweden who believed in *A Good Day to Die*, especially my very devoted publisher, Jennie Sjögren.

To my agents at Nordin Agency, and to Jan Boeje at Buoy Media. Thank you for trying so hard to bring Jim's story to other countries.

And Jesper, the love of my life. Thank you for believing in my stories and me, always. Thank you for loving me in all shapes: victim, survivor, and warrior.

Finally, the biggest thank you to you for reading this. I hope this book helped you in some way.